Entrepreneur
POCKET GUIDES

How to Sell
TOYS AND
HOBBIES
on
eBay

Entrepreneur Press and
J. S. McDougall

EP
Entrepreneur.
Press

Editorial Director: Jere L. Calmes
Cover Design: Beth Hansen-Winter
Production and Composition: Eliot House Productions

This publication is designed to provide accurate and authoritative information in regard to the subject matter covered. It is sold with the understanding that the publisher is not engaged in rendering legal, accounting or
other professional services. If legal advice or other expert assistance is
required, the services of a competent professional person should be sought.

Library of Congress Cataloging-in-Publication Data is available.
    McDougall, J. S.
    How to sell toys and hobbies on eBay/by J.S. McDougall.
       p.   cm.
    ISBN-13: 978-1-59918-006-9 (alk. paper)
    ISBN-10: 1-59918-006-5 (alk. paper)
       1. Toy industry—Vocational guidance. 2. Hobby equipment indus-
    try—Vocational guidance. 3. Internet auctions. 4. eBay (Firm) I. Title.
    HD9993.T692M37 2006
    381'.45688720688—dc22   2006004271

Printed in Canada
12 11 10 09 08 07 06   10 9 8 7 6 5 4 3 2 1

Contents

Preface

*T*he story is common. It's 10 P.M. on a Monday night. You're trapped in a company-wide corporate training session listening to a lecture on the virtues of TPS Reports and "positive and specific corrective feedback." Your chair is uncomfortable, your stomach is empty, and you're faced with the horror of repeating this every day for a week. While staring at the flickering fluorescent lights, you are struck with two thoughts: throwing your shoe at the speaker is probably not a good idea, and the time has finally come to start your own business. You throw your shoe, and leave.

If this story sounds familiar, you're in good company. Throngs of people, just like you, are searching for, and finding, better ways to make ends meet, earn extra cash, and maybe even strike it rich. Advances in Internet technology makes it possible for Lil' Ol' You to instantly connect with millions of people. If you have a good idea for a business and a solid plan for growth, there's no limit to how large—and profitable—your idea can become.

Setting up on the internet with your own web site presents real advantages: your products are immediately available to anyone with an internet connection; e-promotion can be cheap and efficient; and automated payment processing simplifies finances. However, running your own web site is not without its own set of challenges: building web site traffic can be complicated; strict security measures must be taken to protect customers; and maintaining a large website is, in itself, a full-time job.

Luckily for us, eBay has addressed many of these challenges. eBay provides the website. eBay provides the payment processing. eBay provides the rigorous marketing. And eBay provides over 100 million potential customers right to your virtual doorstep. For these reasons, and many more, eBay is a great place to start your business.

eBay was developed by Pierre Omidyar in 1995 with the idea that it would be an internet site to help individuals buy and sell items online. But, after product resellers, retailers, and manufacturers learned of eBay's many virtues, it quickly grew to become the world's marketplace that it is today. More than 100 million people are currently a part of the eBay community and over 1 billion items are sold on eBay every year. While the market potential is staggering, the task of grabbing the attention of, and then successfully selling to, that market is not easily accomplished. You will have many competitors, and obstacles, along the road to becoming a PowerSeller. This book will provide you with the tools necessary to begin selling toys and hobby items at a rate you never thought possible while sitting in corporate training sessions taking aim with your shoe.

For Mom and Dad, my foundation in this world.

CHAPTER 1

Charting
the Water

*W*HAT COULD BE MORE FUN THAN SELLING YOUR favorite toys for a living? Who wouldn't want to expand a favorite hobby into a lucrative career? Thousands of people are doing exactly that and enjoying every minute of it by selling toys and hobby items on eBay. The Toys & Hobbies category is one of eBay's top five most profitable. Parents, collectors, and nostalgic thirtysomethings are buying up most everything that this eBay category has to offer. Many savvy eBay sellers have already recognized and capitalized on eBay's large and hungry toys and hobbies market. With some research, foresight, and careful planning, you can join their ranks.

While selling on eBay is a great way to earn money, it is not a get-rich-quick miracle. Care must be taken when conducting all your transactions and dealing with bidders. eBay's feedback system is a double-edged sword. It will, at once, boast to the world how great a seller you are, while revealing to the world exactly where you are lagging behind. It takes a lot of work to make and keep buyers happy. If you've ever had a job that deals directly with the public, then you know this already. If you do not have the time or interest to devote to taking care of the details of doing business, such as getting packages to the shipping store on time in the middle of a snowstorm, or answering buyer emails after a long day of crunching numbers in your cubicle, then selling on eBay is not for you. Your feedback score will suffer, and soon buyers will shy away from your listings. However, if you're ready and excited for the possibilities eBay presents, then you will have a rewarding and profitable experience.

PowerSelling versus Selling as a Hobby

The first step in selling on eBay is to decide your commitment level to this endeavor. There are two levels of commitment when discussing selling on eBay: hobby seller and PowerSeller. The hobby seller sells casually for extra cash when he finds time in his schedule. The PowerSeller has made selling online his career. The tips found in this book will help both the hobby seller and PowerSeller become more successful, but the initial planning for these two commitment levels is decidedly different. We'll discuss the differences throughout the book, but for now just think carefully about whether you want to depend on selling toys on eBay as your only income, or if you'd like it to supplement what you're already earning elsewhere.

Both hobby selling and PowerSelling can be fun, exciting, and lucrative. If you're not sure where to begin, plan to start small and grow over time. It's much easier to start selling as a hobby to supplement your job than it is to start selling full time and then grovel for your job back if you decide this career isn't for you.

Competition

Of all the possible items to sell, selling toys is a smart choice. Vintage toys are always in high demand, and new toys are coming on to the market every day. However, because these items are immensely popular with bidders, they are also immensely popular with eBay sellers, which means that you will find plenty of competition in this category. Be aware that if you plan to reach the coveted PowerSeller status, you have your work cut out for you. Many PowerSellers are busy not only keeping a careful eye on their own businesses, but they also have learned to keep a strict eye on their competition—you.

The bright side of having a lot of competition is that it provides a lot of opportunities for market research. This is where you should begin your journey to becoming a successful eBay toy seller. Know your competition, both on eBay and off. What are their strengths? More importantly, what are their weaknesses? If your competition sells on eBay, find and study their product listings. Are they attractive, complete, clear? Read their customer feedback comments. Are buyers complaining about slow shipping, inaccurate descriptions, or poor customer service? Find these faults, and make it your goal to provide better service in these areas.

Your off-eBay competition will be more familiar to you. You'll be competing with the national retail chains such as Wal-Mart and Target, along with specialized toy stores such as Kay-Bee Toys and Toys 'R Us. Visit these stores and browse their selections. What can you offer that they don't carry? Can you offer what they do at a better price? Make notes of what you find and incorporate them into your product strategy.

Devising a Product Strategy

eBay's "Toys & Hobbies" is a rather umbrella-like term covering everything from vintage trading cards to stuffed animals to video games. Finding your niche within the category can be quite a task. There are a few considerations that need to be taken before you begin investing in inventory.

New, Used, or Vintage

The Toys & Hobbies category contains items of all ages. It has the latest retail video games, and it has antique rocking horses that predate Seabiscuit. You'll need to think about whether you would like to sell new, used, or vintage items. Each has its advantages and drawbacks.

NEW ITEMS. Selling new items in eBay auctions can be challenging. Most bidders search through auctions expecting to find a bargain. In fact, most auctions of new items sell for only around 20 percent off retail price. Above that, bidders decide it is worth it to buy the item locally for a few bucks more. So profit margins can be slim.

Selling new items in an eBay Store, however, is another matter. Toy stores abound on eBay where prices are retail and items are squeaky clean. Once bidders move past auctions and into a seller's eBay Store, the shopper's expectations shift. No longer are prices fluid. They are fixed prices on fixed inventories. Now, normal retail prices are no longer seen as an offense, they are expected. Many PowerSellers sell over 90 percent of their items from their eBay store, simply because the fixed prices allow them to guarantee suitable profits on every sale.

One major advantage to selling new toys and hobby items is the ease of sourcing items. New items have active product lines. They are still in production, and moving along traditional product channels from manufacturer, to distributor, to wholesaler, to retailer, to end consumer. Finding and buying items at any point along this chain can be easier and less time consuming than scouring a thousand garage sales looking for one out-of-production Beanie Baby. See Chapter 4 for more about finding inventory.

Demand for new items depends, of course, on the item. Like in the rest of the retail world, items that don't catch a buyer's attention simply don't sell. Be sure you have done your homework and are ready to capitalize on the market's trends and mainstays.

USED ITEMS. Used, nonvintage, items have some significant advantages over selling new items. For one, they're less expensive to buy. Auctions, second-hand stores, and estate sales are often full of old toys that just need a quick wash to restore them to selling condition. If you don't mind scrubbing chewing gum off plastic, or throwing stuffed animals in the wash, selling used toys may be for you.

In order to make a profit selling used toys for low prices, you'll need to operate in volume. PowerSeller pawpawrick, whom you'll meet in Chapter 2, does a healthy $1,250/week selling used toys, but he accomplishes that by selling over 600 items per month. If you don't mind high turnover being the driving force behind high revenues, this might be a good way to go.

One of the disadvantages to selling used toys is that you won't have the luxury of steady supply. In order to keep your shelves stocked, you will need to be constantly searching for new inventory.

VINTAGE ITEMS. The main advantage to selling vintage items is that there seems to be a collector in the world for anything. If you're considering selling vintage items, chances are that you're a collector in some form already. Most anything vintage is in high demand, and therefore can produce high profits. Established franchise toys, such as Radio Flyer wagons, Flintstones figures, and McDonald's Premiums are reliably profitable.

Expertise is a must when dealing in vintage items. Bidders and buyers expect an item's seller to be able to answer their questions. For example, if you're selling vintage board games, you'll be expected to know how many pieces were in the original set, and if any are missing. You'll be expected to know what year the game was published, and by what company. If you have a driving passion for a specific toy in history, selling vintage toys is a good idea. If you're unsure about the idea, consider selling new or used toys.

Sell What You Know

As mentioned briefly above, you should sell items you know something about, not simply for the sake of being able to answer your customer's questions, but also for yourself. PowerSeller maximum_thrash put it this way, "I would rather sell something that I have an interest in and enjoy, than just buying and selling something because I can make money doing so, but have no real knowledge or interest in." And he's right. If you are unenthusiastic about your products, your new business will become a chore. Your mood and morale will suffer and eventually the business will bore you. PowerSeller toysheik reinforces this point, "Sell what you know and what you enjoy. Sell anything and everything related to your passion." You'll be glad you did.

Recognizing Opportunity

Some toys will always be in demand, some are tied to market fluctuations, and some are just a quick flash-in-the-pan. But even a flash-in-the-pan can produce respectable profits. Think of the Cabbage Patch phenomenon in the 1980s. Or, the Beanie Baby craze in the 1990s. Tickle-Me-Elmo? Whatever it is that you decide to sell, it will help you to keep your eye on what's coming.

CONSTANT DEMAND. Some items will forever be in high demand. This could be because they have reached icon status within our culture, or because the people they represent have, or simply because they will always be fun to play with.

Some sports toys, such as Michael Jordan dolls, Larry Bird figures, Walter Payton footballs, will always have a home on eBay. Collectors and fans around the world have an insatiable appetite for the symbols of their heroes.

Iconic American toys, such as the Radio Flyer wagon, Mickey Mouse dolls, and G.I. Joes have attained a level of popularity bordering on fame. These toys are instantly recognizable to millions of people, and therefore have large potential for profits. Beware of knock-offs or replicas. Collectors of these items will not stand for second rate.

Some of the most profitable toys on eBay are less specialized than you may think. Simple yo-yos, model trains, and LEGO sets are, and will always be, incredibly fun to play with. Don't underestimate fun as a marketing tool. MGMagic sells simple magic tricks to parents and children all over the country. He enjoys a steady stream of sales without depending on vintage status or iconic collectibles.

SHOPPING TRENDS. There are the normal shopping trends that we're all familiar with, such as holiday shopping and tax-return season. These are easy to capitalize on as we all see them coming like a freight train. But then, again, all your competitors see them coming as well. And therefore, you may not be gaining any ground during these sales booms, just keeping up.

In order to get ahead of your competition, you'll need to watch for more subtle shopping trends that apply specifically to your products. Sometimes, you'll be blind-sided by trends that you could not have predicted—such as the Po, the defective Teletubby incident of 1998. But others you can see coming, if you know where to look.

There are certain franchise toys that pop up every few years. Spider-Man was in a long lull of obscurity until the recent release of the Tobey Maguire movies revitalized the Spidey franchise. The recent release of the Dukes of Hazzard movie brought back demand for the General Lee. At the time of this printing, Superman is experiencing a lull in popularity, but has a movie due out later this year. Now would be a good time to gobble up vintage, used, and new Superman toys. When the movie is released in a few months, the country's appetite for the Caped Crusader will grow tremendously. Wouldn't it be wonderful to have a warehouse full of Superman-related items when the movie launches? Watch the movie studios' announcements. See if there is any potential for the rebirth of toy genres.

Also, if Harry Potter has taught us anything, it's that kids today, in fact, do read. Just like movie releases, blockbusters from the pen of J.K. Rowling re-intensify the demand for Harry Potter items every few years. Watch other current and upcoming children's literature for any fertile ground.

These signals for upcoming trends can come from any major media outlet. Keep an eye on the rebirth of cartoons, TV shows, advertising icons, internet sensations, and so on.

CHAPTER 2

Meet the
PowerSellers

*T*O HELP BRING TO LIGHT THE OPPORTUNITIES AND obstacles of selling toys on eBay, we have interviewed some top sellers in the Toys & Hobbies category. Each of the sellers profiled below has attained PowerSeller status. To become a PowerSeller, a seller must:

- Have been an active seller on eBay for more than 90 days

- List at least four items per month for the last three months

- Reached a feedback level of at least 100 with a 98 percent positive rating

- Generate at least $1,000 per month for at least three months in a row

As you can see, PowerSellers have found strategies that work! And the PowerSellers in this book have been gracious enough to share their time and knowledge with us.

Below is a brief description of each PowerSeller and his or her business. You will also find helpful tips from these sellers in the chapters ahead.

MGMagic

Mike Garrido started selling magic tricks and novelty items on eBay in 2003. Magic had been a hobby of his for many years prior to opening up his own business, so when he decided to try his hand at selling on eBay, magic tricks were his ticket. He operates the business in his spare time from his home in California.

When he first started, Mike took the risk of buying his initial inventory with his personal credit card. He put everything he bought up for auction and was off and running. He hasn't needed to touch his credit card since, as the business was quickly self-sustaining. He reinvests his profits back into the business by buying up more magic tricks, instructional books, and novelty items like his self-inflating whoopee cushions and farting piggy banks. He runs occasional auctions, but mostly sells at fixed prices from his fully stocked eBay Store, Michael G's Magic and Novelty Shop.

He's earned a 100 percent positive feedback rating with well over a thousand transactions in the past 12 months. His customers credit him with being a great communicator, a fast shipper, and a lot of fun to do business with. We believe them—what could be more fun than self-inflating whoopee cushions? It's obvious that Mike has learned a thing or two about doing business on eBay.

www.kryptoys.com

Jason Zlatkus has been selling monster and horror toys for far longer than eBay has been around—over 16 years. He sells only on the internet now, through his own web site and in his eBay store. He admits that he had to be pushed into selling on eBay by some friends who had become sellers before him. It was about nine years ago, he remembers, that his friends guided him through the eBay set-up process. But, soon after that, he got the knack of it and was off and running, selling his terrifyingly ugly masks, puppets, and figures.

He goes by the user ID www.kryptoys.com to draw attention to his independent web site located at both kryptoys.com and cryptoys.com. He works from his home in Oregon where he has dedicated his garage to the business. Like many other sellers, he decided to start the business off small and grow over time. Today, he has over 2,000 transactions under his belt and a 99.5 percent positive feedback rating—1,000 of those transactions taking place within the last 12 months.

maximum_thrash

Dale Shearer started selling on eBay in 2002 when his die-cast toy car collection had grown too large. He started selling with the idea that he'd just offload some of the cars in his collection that he didn't need or want any longer. But, he immediately realized the potential of selling toys on eBay, and used the profits from his initial sales to buy up more of what he found to be the best-selling cars. Within eight months he had enough inventory to open up his eBay Store, ShearerSpeed.

The business is currently a one-man show, he says, but he's growing so fast that he anticipates the day when he'll have to make the decision between staying small or hiring help. He's already outgrown his home and had to rent a storage area from a local business. With over 2,000 items listed in his store, and over 3,000 sales in the last year, it's easy to see why he needed to move out of the basement.

Dale hopes to concentrate on the business full time after his retirement, which, he says, is only a few years away. He has plans to expand and diversify the items he carries, while keeping the die-cast collector cars that he knows and loves as the foundation of his business.

toysheik

When Henry Pagan found himself unsatisfied with his position at a financial firm on Wall Street, he decided he needed to make a change. And what a drastic change he made. He left his job in the city and decided to re-explore his boyhood passion for action figures. He started trading and selling at trade shows and conventions before launching his own web site at www.toysheik.com and selling through auctions on eBay.

Between 1998 and 2004, Henry regarded this eBay adventure as his "little side business." He tried ramping up his business by increasing the number of auctions he posted, but he grew frustrated when the profits were being eaten up by listing and transaction fees. It was then that he decided to try opening up an eBay store to increase his sales and profits. The result, he says, was immediately apparent.

Henry's eBay store now boasts over 3,700 items for sale, which makes his one of the largest action figure stores on eBay. He's got action figures of Austin Powers to Invader Zim and every one in between. Henry has a large following of loyal repeat customers who have peppered his feedback page with words like "awesome" and "excellent" and "perfect." Combine that with his 99.8 percent positive feedback score of 2,863 and over 2,000 sales in the last year, and it seems that leaving Wall Street was the right move.

pawpawrick

As Rick and Joanne Everman see it, they have two jobs. The first is running their successful eBay Store, Kids-n-Mom, which sells toys, stuffed animals, games, and children's books. The second, they tell us, is spoiling their first grandchild. In fact, spoiling their grandson is the reason they got started on eBay in the first place. Upon registering for the site in July of 2003, they did quite a bit of research for, and purchasing of, the best toys, puzzles, and games for the then two-year-old. Three months later they decided to begin selling the toys they had learned so much about, and three months after that, they had achieved PowerSeller status.

Today, they sell over 150 items every week and bring in enough revenue that both Rick and Joanne can work full time on the business. Their eBay Store has over 1,500 items that range from used video games to baby bouncers. Most of what they sell is used and has been found in garage sales, thrift stores, or estate sales. Rick says that all the toys he sells are still perfectly good; they just need a new home with someone to love them. Everything they sell is cleaned up to near-new condition before being shipped off to new owners.

When Rick and Joanne realized the potential of selling toys on eBay, they made a conscientious choice to trade time for money. Joanne left her job as an accountant where she frequently was required to work over 50 hours per week, though made a decent living. Both Rick and Joanne felt that losing her steady income would be worth having more time to enjoy life. And now that the eBay business has grown to a point where it supports them both comfortably, they have no regrets.

mrandjr

Jonathan and Megan Raines began selling action figures on eBay in 2002 to earn some extra income. They were intrigued by eBay and its tenet that an open and transparent marketplace would thrive with the honesty and courtesy of its participants. They've only run into fraud twice in the last four years, and have found eBay's belief to be true. They say that the vast majority of the people they've met on eBay are honest and a pleasure to work with.

Their eBay Store, MJ's Toys and Collectibles, now accounts for 90 percent of their sales and has over 4,000 items. The bulk of their business is 1970s and 1980s action figures, but they also offer nonsports trading cards and sports memorabilia. When they're not tending to their customers, they're off hunting for more vintage figures at toy shows, antique malls, and all types of local auctions.

They work from their home, which due to the business's growth over the years, is beginning to look more like a warehouse. To ensure continued growth, they set monthly profit goals for themselves and are meticulous about organizing their inventory. They hope to become Silver PowerSellers ($3,000 in sales per month) within the year, and, from the look of it, they're well on their way.

Your Turn

This book contains tips and anecdotes from the PowerSellers above about how they run their successful businesses and what you can do to begin yours. They have been gracious enough to donate their time and knowledge to helping you, as is common in the eBay community, and for that we are grateful. The next time you're on eBay, check out their auctions and stores. Click "Advanced Search," "Find A Member," and then search for them by User ID. You're likely to be surprised by how much they've grown since the publication of this book.

With the information in the chapters ahead, you'll learn how to build a business to the level of these PowerSellers. So get excited, and read on. A successful toy store is closer than you think!

CHAPTER 3

The
Logistics

*R*EGISTERING FOR AN EBAY ACCOUNT IS PAINLESS. eBay has done a great job making the process straightforward. And while it may be technically easy, there are some steps that require careful consideration before submission.

To begin the process, click the Register link on eBay.com's main page. You will see a progress bar across the top of the page with the three steps in the registration process: Enter Information, Choose User ID & Password, and Check Your Email. You will also see a link for Live Help at the top of the page. Clicking this link will produce a chat window that connects you with a member of the eBay customer service team. If you get stuck during this process, or find yourself with a question, click this link for help.

Enter Your Information

Enter your personal information into the appropriate text boxes on this page. Be sure to double check your information for accuracy, as this will be the information used to conduct business and people need to trust that it is correct.

User Agreement and Privacy Policy

Most people never take the time to read the User Agreements or Privacy Policies of the sites they join. In most cases, this practice in harmless. But in this case, we strongly suggest you read through eBay's User Agreement. It states, in no uncertain terms, the infractions that will get you kicked out of the eBay community and banned from selling on the site. Not all of the infractions are obvious, and some make it quite conceivable that an unsuspecting new user could break one of them relatively easily. Realizing down the road that you have failed to abide by eBay's User Agreement can put an immediate end to your income. It has happened to unsuspecting sellers many times. Please read the User Agreement. Below are some forbidden actions that often trip up new users, with our comments.

While using the site, you will not:

- post content or items in an inappropriate category or areas on the site. (With something as simple as a missed click of the mouse, a user could mistakenly post an item to an inappropriate category. Be sure to double check.)

- manipulate the price of any item or interfere with other user's listings. (It is tempting and easy to bid on your own items to boost the sale price, but the practice is strictly forbidden.)

- distribute or post spam, chain letters, or pyramid schemes. (When the excitement of owning a new business strikes, many new users are tempted to contact as many people as possible to advertise their services. It may not seem so at the time, but this is spamming. It is not allowed through eBay's e-mail forms, in the discussion boards, or from any other contact information collected from eBay's site.)

eBay's User Agreement also contains a very clear Content License clause, which states:

> When you give us content, you grant us a non-exclusive, worldwide, perpetual, irrevocable, royalty-free, sub-licensable (through multiple tiers) right to exercise the copyright, publicity, and database rights (but no other rights) you have in the content, in any media known now or in the future. (We need these rights to host and display your content.)

So, in other words, don't post the text of your upcoming novel as the description of an item, because once you do, eBay owns it.

In addition to these points, there are quite a few additional important facets of the User Agreement that should be known to every seller. Read it.

Choose User ID and Password

Choosing the right User ID is important for all sellers. This User ID will be how people identify you and your business on eBay. Casual sellers have the luxury of considering variations of their own names as User IDs, while more ambitious sellers do not. The User ID of your eBay business should be short, memorable, easily pronounced, and appropriate for your product line, while leaving room for later growth. For example, a seller of Magic: The Gathering cards should choose a name that identifies the business as a seller of trading card games, but doesn't rule out growth into selling Harry Potter cards, Lord of the Rings cards, and Yu-Gi-Oh cards in the future. "MagicTGCards" would be a poor choice, while "TradingCardTraders" will serve them better down the road. Also, more obviously, choose a User ID that is appropriate for the type of items you will be selling. "TeddyBearLuv" would not be an appropriate User ID for a seller of remote-controlled cars, while adorable, it is misleading.

You may be asked to confirm your identity by entering a credit or debit card number. This is a safety measure to ensure you are over 18 years of age and have a valid mailing address. Your card will not be charged at this time.

Check Your E-Mail

Once you have submitted all your information to eBay and chosen your User ID, you will be sent an e-mail asking you to confirm your registration. This e-mail will contain a confirmation code that you will need to enter into eBay's registration confirmation page. This e-mail and confirmation code validates that the e-mail address you entered is valid and that you have access to it. Follow the instructions in the confirmation e-mail and you will have completed your eBay registration.

Now, to begin selling, you will need to register as a seller. Click the Start Selling link on the page that results from clicking the link in your registration confirmation e-mail. You will be asked to enter a credit or debit card number to place on file. This is, again, just a security measure to confirm your age, name, and address. You card will not be charged.

You will next be asked to input account and routing information for a checking account. This is a measure eBay takes to ensure that they will be able to collect the seller's fees if the credit or debit card you've provided expires. As the last step in this process you must select the method by which to pay your seller's fees (from the card you've just placed on file, or the bank account).

Account Set Up

Now that you're all set up with a seller account, the first order of business is to get your account set up with some necessary information. We will cover a few of the most important items here, but we can't cover everything, so it will be up to you to work your way down the options provided in the My Account menu on the left side of your My eBay page.

Your About Me Page

The content of your About Me page is entirely up to you, and therefore gives you the opportunity to tell eBay buyers about yourself, your business, and your products. Most sellers use this page as a place to introduce themselves, put up some photos, lay out their shipping and payment policies, and perhaps link to a few of their auctions. If done well, your About Me page will show some personality, give buyers a sense of familiarity, and drive sales.

To begin setting up your About Me page, log into your account, click Personal Information under the My Account menu on the left side of the page. On the resulting page, you are able to edit all the personal information associated with your account. Click Edit next to the About Me page option.

There are two methods available to you for setting up an About Me page: through eBay's step-by-step process or by entering your own HTML code. Writing your own HTML code allows for more customization than the step-by-step process, but is only recommended for sellers who are comfortable writing HTML. This page is not a place where novice coders should cut their teeth. It must have a professional appearance to reflect your business advantageously.

The step-by-step process will ask for a page title, some text, and some photographs. You can also display your recent sales history, and provide links to helpful web sites. This is the only page on which eBay will allow you to post off-eBay links, so do so wisely. Post links to web sites that will be helpful to your buyers. For example, posting a link to a Tips for Model Builders page will help your buyers get more out of your model train collections, but posting a link to photos of your grandmother's lovable dog, Rapscallion, will not.

When writing text for your About Me page you should consider including your business mailing address and telephone number. Buyers like to see that you are willing to provide real-world avenues for support. This is an easy way to immediately boost your buyers' confidence. However, if you work from home, and do not yet have a business mailing address and business-specific telephone line, you may not want to list your personal information. There's no limit to the amount of frustration one cranky customer armed with your home telephone number can cause. You should, however, prominently post an e-mail address here to receive bidders' questions.

Once you have inserted all your information and configured your options, you then select a layout, preview your page, and submit.

Selling Preferences

From your My eBay page, click Preferences in the My Account menu. You will see a host of options that you should explore and set to your liking. In this preferences panel you are able to configure almost every facet of your eBay account, from which newsletters you receive to how you accept payments from buyers. This is also the first place you will be asked about PayPal.

Personal Checks and Money Orders

When accepting personal checks and money orders from buyers you should wait a few days to make sure the funds arrive in your account before making the shipment. Sometimes, whether intended by the buyer or not, personal checks will

PAYPAL

PayPal enables people to send and receive money online. Having a PayPal account is similar to having a checking account at your local bank. You can deposit money to your PayPal account from your personal bank account, you can withdraw money from your PayPal account in various ways, including electronic transfer to your personal bank account, and you can send money from your PayPal account to any person with an e-mail address. PayPal made sending money online so easy that it quickly became the default method buyers used to pay for their eBay purchases. It became so widely used on eBay, in fact, that in late 2002, eBay bought PayPal and began further integrating PayPal's services into its own.

Today, PayPal is ubiquitous among eBay auctions. Nearly every seller on eBay has a PayPal account on which they can receive payments from buyers. Not only does PayPal make sending money easier for buyers, it also provides sellers with the ability to accept instant payments, to accept major credit cards, and to avoid bounced checks and fraudulent money orders. It is not uncommon that only seconds after the end of an auction full payment has been delivered by the buyer to the seller's PayPal account—making the entire transaction easier for everyone.

One of the downsides of PayPal is that some buyers find it too risky a proposition to submit their sensitive financial information, such as bank account numbers and credit card information, when registering for a PayPal account. They, therefore, refuse to sign up for a PayPal account. For this reason, making your auctions "PayPal only" will alienate some potential buyers. You should be willing to accept other forms of payment from your buyers such as personal checks or money orders.

■   ■   ■

bounce, leaving you with the hassle of contacting the buyer and collecting payment. Also, a popular method of defrauding sellers on eBay is to send a counterfeit money order for the payment amount. You can and should protect yourself from these scams by waiting to ship any items. Make clear to buyers on each of your items' auction pages that if the buyer intends to use one of these two forms of payment that the shipping will be delayed while waiting for funds to clear.

My eBay

The next step to setting up your eBay sellers account is to familiarize yourself with your My eBay page. This screen will function as your eBay control panel. It provides up-to-the-minute information concerning all your dealings on eBay: items on which you're bidding; items you're selling; messages from eBay and others in the community; and all your preferences. After you've just opened your eBay account, this page will be fairly sparse. But as soon as you become an active eBay community member, this page will burst to life. To help you get that process started, Chapter 4 discusses where to search for items to sell in your very own eBay auctions.

Inventory
Resources

*O*NE OF THE MOST CLOSELY GUARDED SECRETS OF AN eBay PowerSeller is from where they source their items. It is hard to get a straight answer out of sellers on the topic, and that's just as it should be. Asking a PowerSeller for her product source secrets is like asking Aunt Berta for her secret cookie recipe—you can ask, but you risk being chased by an aggressive rolling pin.

The PowerSellers we spoke to told us that they continuously search for new sources of items. They search every step of the product life chain, from manufacturers to liquidators. And when they find a great source for items, they do all they can to protect and nurture that relationship. A good item source serves as the foundation for building a reliable and profitable business.

As every PowerSeller does, you will also need to do your own research of item sources. Below we've put together some great places to start your search, and a few things to look for in a good source.

New Items

The source of your items depends largely on what you plan to sell. An eBay seller of new Sesame Street toys will have different sources than a seller of used playground equipment. So begin with a clear idea of what you plan to sell. If you plan to sell new items, make a list of the retailers and manufacturers that you know of in that product line. From that list you can begin to trace your way up and down the product's life-chain to find the best place to buy. For example, if you are planning to sell new Play-Doh sets, the product's life-chain would look similar to this:

- manufacturer (Hasbro)
- distributor (Entertainment Earth, etc.)
- wholesaler (CostCo, etc.)
- retailer (Target, etc.)
- liquidator (liquidation.com, etc.)

Pick up the phone and call around to find the sale prices, policies, and restrictions at every step in the chain. Keep in mind that with every successive step in the chain away from the manufacturer, another middleperson is added and the price goes up. So start with the manufacturer and work your way down.

Manufacturers

More often than not, large manufacturers are set up (both physically and financially) to move products down the product life chain by the truckload, and are unwilling to take the time to sell in smaller quantities or deal with individual sales altogether. This makes buying directly from the manufacturer difficult. However, manufacturers also occasionally run into the problem of having too much inventory of an older item, which can take up valuable space in a warehouse. When on the phone with the manufacturer, be sure to ask if they have any overstocked, or "dead-stock," items that you could help them to liquidate. You'll be doing them a favor by clearing space for their new items, and you'll be getting a good deal on older, but unused, items.

Distributors

When speaking to an item's manufacturer, be sure to ask for its distributors. Call the distributors and ask them if you can become a reseller. They may require you to buy in large quantities or pay huge shipping costs, which may or may not work for your business model, but it could provide you with a great source if you can make it work. Be sure to crunch some numbers before you pick up the phone. Also, if you determine that you can, in fact, buy a truckload of See 'n Says, be sure that you have the ability to store, sell, and track that amount of inventory. See more about inventory concerns in Chapter 12.

Wholesalers

Wholesale clubs such as CostCo and Sam's Club should not be overlooked just because they are available to the general shopping public. They fall victim to the same problems of overstocking that many manufacturers run into. You may find deep discounts on desirable items sitting on the warehouse shelves just down the road from you. Just because an item isn't selling in your neck of the woods does not mean that there isn't high demand for it somewhere among the millions of eBay shoppers. Stick with trusted wholesalers, as most require a membership fee and some could turn out to be scammers.

Retailers

Buying from retailers only makes sense when you can get a deal. Often sellers will find great deals from local retailers by buying up their customer returns. Some large retailers find it cheaper to destroy customer returns than to diagnose, fix, and restock them. So whether an item comes back to them because it is faulty, or just because it was an unwanted gift, the item is destroyed and the retailer absorbs the loss. By buying up customer returns, you get your items at a price significantly lower than retail, and the retailer recoups some loss. Just be aware that customer-returned items are often faulty, and cannot be sold as new or reconditioned items without some repair. It may or may not be worth your time to test and repair items before reselling them.

Another option when sourcing from retailers is to buy their dead stock. Many retailers provide an outlet for their old goods as a way to clean off their shelves and recoup some losses from unsold merchandise. Ask the large retailers in your area if they have such a program.

Liquidators

Many PowerSellers buy their items through liquidation, which is the last step in a new product's life chain. Items that are never sold to an end-consumer are liquidated for a fraction of the retail price, often in bulk. You will find pallets of mostly old and damaged items up for sale—sometimes all mixed in together. There are great deals to be had, for sure, but be careful when buying from liquidation companies. Most sell used goods from companies that are going out of business, or returned items from retail stores. If you're not careful about what you're buying, and from what company, you might end up stuck with a

> "My items come from all over: wholesale companies, trade shows, other collectors, and even some from eBay itself."
>
> —cryptoys

pallet load of damaged goods that are hard, or even impossible, to sell.

Used Items

If you are planning on selling used items, you will need to follow a path different than those seeking new items. Your path will be a little less formal, a little more fun, and a little closer to home. The disadvantage to selling used items is that steady, reliable sources for quality items are hard to find. Steady sources of used items, such as the retail customer returns, as mentioned in the previous section, and liquidation services such as liquidation.com may provide you with a steady stream of items, though it will occasionally be polluted by faulty and unsalable toys.

Garage Sales

Search for garage sales listed in your local classifieds, on bulletin boards, and along the roadsides in your area. Attend the sales in an order based on the likelihood that they will have toys for sale. Start with affluent suburbs, and established neighborhoods with aging parents looking to clean out some rooms. New neighborhoods tend to have young families who are just starting out,

> "The magic wholesalers that I work with are the best in their line of business. I found their contact information in magic publications that I subscribe to."
>
> —MGMagic

and tend not to have too much of value to sell. Or, they need their toys for the crop of newborns. While searching in the papers for garage sales, keep an eye out for estate sales and moving sales as well.

Local Auctions

Auctions, whether offered by a private organization or by the government, can be great places to find lots of toys. Auction houses often sell off donated toys from local closet cleaners.

> "Over time I needed more cars than I could find at toy shows, so I started searching the internet and found some wholesalers that I could buy from. I had bought such a large amount of cars from one wholesaler that I was contacted by the car manufacturer. Now I buy from them."
>
> —maximum_thrash

These auctions are advertised in the local media, and occur fairly regularly. Call ahead to find out what type of items will be up for auction, and if the auction consists of a decent amount of items that you can sell in your store, it might be worth attending. Though, be sure when bidding to keep your profit margin in mind. Don't let yourself get sucked into the bidding frenzy that makes auctions so successful. You could end up with the perfect item at too high a price to produce any profits for you.

Newspaper Advertising

If after all the searching and running around, you're getting tired of chasing inventory, why not let the merchandise come

> "The vast majority of the items we sell are vintage and no longer available through retail stores or wholesalers. Locating quality pieces is a little challenging. We spend countless hours traveling to toys shows, antique malls, and all types of auctions. We also do a lot of shopping on several web sites. One of our main sources of product is through purchasing private collections."
>
> —mrandjr

to you? You've probably seen ads in your local classifieds saying something akin to, "Cash For Antique Toys!" or "We pay cash for your old toys!" They are there because they work. Place your phone number and e-mail address in the paper with a description of the type of items you're looking to buy, and people will start contacting you. This method will not provide you with all of your inventory, but, every so often, it will send a few dolls or trading cards or rocking horses your way, saving you time and money.

Once you've grown large enough to handle sizable inventories, consider placing ads in larger classified markets and appropriate toy collector magazines.

Buy Smart

Now that you've got a few good places to begin your hunt for toys to sell, you should begin to think about how to buy smart. Going out and buying all the old toys, new toys, or collectibles you can find will not produce a profitable business. It will fill your basement and empty your bank accounts. Before you begin buying, you must first find out what items are selling, and at what price. Then, once you've got an idea of what will fly off the shelf and what will collect dust on it, you can take your knowledge and begin searching in the places listed above for the best-selling stuff, at the prices that will make you a profit.

The first place to begin is on eBay itself. Do a search of completed auctions, under the Advanced Search link on any page, for items similar to what you would like to sell. Take note of final sale price, the number of bids received, and the number of listings for this specific, or similar, items. Consider an item that received eight or more bids to be a "Hot Item," meaning that there is significant demand for that item and the market could bear more like it for sale. If you find multiple completed listings for an item, each of which has eight or more bids, you've found an item worth selling. Your task then becomes to find that item, or the parts to build such an item, at a price that will produce profits when sold at the average sale price of the items in your search.

"We sell items that have been purchased at second-hand stores, garage sales, thrift stores, and estate sales. We do purchase some new "in the box" items from retail establishments—we watch for sales and mainly visit these only during the holiday season."

—pawpawrick

If you find an item that is heavily in demand and are able to list hundreds of that particular item, the average sales price will plummet, leaving you with little, if any, profits and a flooded market. Introduce your products slowly. There is a delicate balance of supply and demand, especially in the microcosm of an eBay category. Increase the number of your listings while keeping an eye fixed on the dropping average sale price of your products. Experiment with the balance between items sold per month and average sale price per item. You will find a point of maximum profitability.

If the item you're considering selling has many listings with less than eight, or zero, bids, you should either consider a different item, or a new approach to selling that item. The harsh reality is that not everything you want to sell will sell. If your dream is to build and sell wicker trampolines, you're likely to be disappointed.

There are many free and commercial tools available to sellers to help them decide what to begin selling. eBay even has some of its own. See Chapter 10 for helpful product research tools.

Listing
Items

*F*INALLY, IT IS TIME TO BEGIN SELLING. THIS CHAPTER
will fill you in on the best ways to get your
toys and hobby items listed, seen, and sold. eBay
is best known for its auctions, but provides other ways to sell as
well. We'll begin with explaining how to list your items in an eBay
auction, but we'll also explain eBay Stores and Fixed Price
Listings—both of which provide great opportunities for sellers to
move more toys.

Auctions

To begin selling, click the Sell tab at the top of the main eBay page.
You will be presented with a few options here, the number of which

will depend on your feedback rating. Sellers with higher feedback ratings are presented with more selling options. First-timers are presented with Online Auction and Real Estate. Choose Online Auction, and continue.

Categories

You will be presented with a large list of item categories from which to choose. For the purposes of selling toys and hobby items, the appropriate category for your auction is Toys & Hobbies.

Before continuing with Toys & Hobbies, take a moment to browse through the lengthy list of eBay top-level categories. You might come across a category that strikes your fancy, and could lead you to another business opportunity. That dusty box in the attic filled with Great-Grandma's scary stuffed bear collection could fetch a hefty paycheck in the lesser-known Dolls & Bears category.

Once you have clicked Toys & Hobbies, scroll down to select a second category for your auction if you wish. Choosing a second category for your auction will increase traffic to your listing, and ultimately it could raise your final sale price. However, don't be tempted to list your item in an inappropriate second category just for the sake of increasing traffic. Listing auctions in inappropriate categories violates the eBay User Agreement and comes with harsh penalties. In most cases, one category is sufficient.

Subcategories

Now you must select a more specific subcategory of the top-level Toys & Hobbies category. The subcategory you choose will depend on the item you're selling. You will be presented with a number of interactive menus that will help you narrow down your category choice to a specific subcategory. Choose, in every menu, the description that best fits your item. The menus will stop expanding once you have reached the most specific subcategory possible.

Choosing all these specifics helps eBay place your item into a category where it will be best found by buyers searching for your item. Choosing these subcategories carefully and correctly will improve your item's chances of being shown to the most interested buyers. Therefore, the item's chances of being sold, and of being sold at a good price, partly depend on your selections here.

For example, say that a fictional seller, Joshua, has inherited an enormous collection of Ty Beanie Babies that he'd like to sell off. He would select Beanbag Plush, Beanie Babies in the first menu and then the most appropriate option in the second menu. He knows that all the items in his collection are genuine Ty products, and therefore selects Ty in the second menu. In the third he selects Beanie Babies to specify the collection type, and then Retired in the fourth menu to specify their age. The last menu asks Joshua to specify an animal type, but because his attic is full, he selects "mixed lots."

In another example, David has chosen to buy and sell action figures. He has just received a pallet of liquidated Spawn figures and is in the process of listing some on eBay. His job is easy. He simply chooses, in successive menus, Action Figures—Spawn. The rest of the menus turn gray and prompt David to continue.

Below the interactive menus, you will again be presented with the opportunity to choose a second top-level category. If you do now wish to choose another category, click continue.

Pre-Filling Information

For many items from major manufacturers, eBay will present you with an option to use its Pre-filled Information. This helpful feature will automatically fill in your item's auction listing with the manufacturer's default information for that particular model or product. If you happen to be selling a toy or board game that eBay has already collected information on, you can take advantage of this option. Most toys, however, won't offer this option.

Standard Listing

Joshua's Beanie Baby collection and David's Spawn collection would not be eligible for the Pre-filled Information option, and they would need to provide all the pertinent information about their lot by hand. Most of the items you put up for auction will need to be listed in a similar way. Once you skip the Pre-filled Information option, you will be presented with the page where you insert the item's title and description.

Title and Description

The importance of writing effective titles and descriptions cannot be understated. Later in this book we will go into detail about what constitutes an effective title and description. But for the purpose of this logistics chapter, we'll give you a brief overview.

Item Title

An auction title is limited to only 55 characters. A character is defined as any letter, number, symbol, or space. The primary function of the title is to clearly state for bidders exactly what the item is that's up for auction. The secondary function of the title is to provide eBay's search program with the keywords it will use to display your auction in user searches. Balancing these two functions, while remaining under the 55-character limit, can be tricky. We'll provide you with some tips on how best to do this in Chapter 7.

Item Subtitle

If you have a hard time fitting all the necessary information into your item's title, you can purchase the use of a subtitle for 50 cents. The item subtitle has the same limit of 55 characters that the item title has, but the text in the subtitle is not included in eBay's search program. So be sure to fit all the critical search terms into the main title because any text you enter into the subtitle field will only serve to provide additional information to bidders.

PowerSellers sometimes use the subtitle to advertise additional noncritical information about the auction, such as low shipping charges, or to boast about their customer feedback scores.

Item Specifics

If your item was originally made by a major manufacturer such as Hasbro or Mattel, chances are that eBay will provide you with an opportunity to detail your item's specifics. If you're listing some Hot Wheels, you'll be asked to specify the item's brand, type, material, scale, year of release, and condition. If you're listing a radio-controlled vehicle, you'll be asked to specify vehicle type, it's sub-type, fuel source, brand, and condition. Specifying these details about your item will help eBay to place it appropriately in search results, which only works to your advantage.

Many types of toys have this Item Specifics option available, while quite a few do not. Don't be surprised if the item you're listing does not present you with this option.

Item Description

The auction description allows you more freedom than the title. There is no character limit, and the description box accepts plain text and HTML. Beginning users should use simple plain text format for the first few auctions, just to get the hang of setting up simple auctions. Plain text will look just like a simple text document. It will suffice as you're getting started, but you will want to become familiar with HTML so that you are able to take advantage of the immense formatting benefits it provides. For tips on how to use HTML in your listings, click on the HTML Tips link below the description text box.

We'll cover how to create effective and stunning description pages in Chapter 7. For now, you should write out the basic information regarding your item. Include the model number (if available), series number, the condition, the manufacturer, and anything else you can think to include. The more information you provide, the less time you'll spend answering e-mails from bidders.

Pricing and Duration

On the next page you will be asked to provide the various prices, auction duration, and photos for your item's listing. There are strategies to each of these pieces of your auction, which will be covered in Chapters 5 and 6. In this chapter, we will focus on defining the terminology used on this page.

Starting Price

The auction's starting price is the amount you set to be the minimum opening bid. If your item sells, it will sell for at least the amount you enter here. The safest strategy is to enter the lowest amount you would be willing to accept for the item. See Chapter 6 for more advanced pricing strategies.

Reserve Price

Setting a reserve price is optional. If set, the amount entered here will act as a safety net for sellers. If bidding does not reach the amount you set for the reserve price, you are not obligated to sell your item. When a reserve price is set, bidders are notified of that fact on the auction's page, though the amount of the reserve price is hidden to encourage bidding.

Buy It Now Price

The Buy It Now price, or BIN, is a price you can offer to buyers who might want to forego the bidding process and purchase the item immediately. Once a bidder chooses to pay your BIN price, the auction ends. Setting a BIN price is a good idea as it opens up your item to a new market of convenience buyers who do not like to participate in bidding, and are happy to pay a higher price to receive the item sooner.

Donate Percentage of Sale

eBay's Giving Works program allows you to dictate whether or not you would like to donate a portion of the item's ultimate sale price to charity, and, if so, what percentage. If you choose to donate some of your proceeds to charity, eBay will present you with hundreds of nonprofit organizations from which to choose. After selecting an organization from the list and selecting the percentage of the sale price you would like to donate, eBay will handle the rest.

Duration

Seven days is the standard length of an eBay auction. You are able to choose from one-, three-, five-, and seven-day listings for the standard listing fee. If you would like your auction to run for ten days, eBay will charge you an extra 40 cents. Most PowerSellers use the standard seven-day auction. Auctions are easier to keep track of when you can plan on an auction ending exactly one week from when you submitted it.

Fixed Price Listings

Technically, a fixed price listing is not an auction because there is no bidding, but those listings show up in auction search results. This format allows users to buy and sell items immediately at a set price, with no bidding or waiting. You can sell more than one of an item in a fixed price listing, which saves you time and money in listing fees.

Private Listing

Private listings are available for sellers who require anonymity for their bidders during an auction. During a private auction, bidders' user IDs are not displayed on the auction's page or in the bidding history. Only the seller can view the IDs of the different bidders. Setting up a private auction may be appropriate for high-priced items, or items that are so in demand that a buyer would benefit from remaining anonymous.

Start Time

The day and time that your auction ends depends on when your auction begins and the duration you have set. There are two ways to dictate when your auction will end. First, you can submit your auction at the specific time of day that you would like the auction to end, and, when the duration you have set expires, it will end accordingly. Or, for an additional 10 cents, eBay allows you to schedule the time your auction will start, thereby freeing you to submit your auction whenever you have time.

Most bidding on any particular auction occurs within the last few minutes. This is because as an auction nears its end, it moves up in eBay's auction list when it is sorted in the default "Time: ending soonest" order. Also, savvy bidders have learned not to place bids early in order to prevent other bidders from outbidding them. Rather, they wait until the final few seconds of an auction to place their maximum bid. This way, they keep the final sale price low and improve their chances of sneaking in the last bid. This practice is called "sniping."

Due to sniping, PowerSellers make a point of ending their auctions during eBay's peak traffic times. Auctions that end during peak hours receive substantially more bids due to the higher number of bidders on the site to see their auction when it is at the top of the list. As a general rule, Sunday evenings, between 6 P.M. and midnight (EST) tend to be eBay's highest traffic times. There are exceptions, of course, such as Super Bowl Sunday when eBay traffic, and internet traffic as a whole, plummets.

Quantity

eBay allows sellers to post auctions that have one or more items for sale. If you are selling one item only, you will not need to specify a quantity. If you are selling multiple items, there are several ways to do so.

INDIVIDUAL ITEMS. If you wish to sell more than one of an identical item, eBay allows you to specify a quantity for an auction provided you meet the following requirements. You must be:

- ID verified
- or have a feedback rating of 30 or more and have been registered on eBay for more than 14 days
- or have a PayPal account, accept PayPal payments, and have a feedback score of 15 or higher

Multiple-item auctions work differently than single-item auctions. Bidders submit their offered price and the number of items they wish to purchase. The winning bid has the highest total price, which equals the offered price multiplied by the number of items requested. All winning bidders pay the lowest successful offered price.

LOTS. If you would like to sell many items in one bunch instead of piecing them out separately, you can sell them as a single lot. You will need to specify the number of identical items that are in the lot and provide a description of the items. Bidders will bid on the lot as a whole instead of for one individual item. The winning bidder takes them all.

Item Location

This address should be set to the location from which you do your shipping. It is used by buyers to calculate accurate shipping costs, which many bidders smartly factor into their bids.

Add Pictures

Pictures are critical pieces of your auction. Auctions without photos sell poorly, or not at all. Bidders like to see the items on which they're bidding. eBay provides two methods for placing photos in your auctions. Sellers can use eBay's own Basic Picture Services, or a third-party web host.

EBAY BASIC PICTURE SERVICES. If you choose to use eBay's picture services, your first photo is included in the listing price. Every additional photo you choose to insert costs 15 cents. To upload photos using this service, simply click the "Browse" button and locate the appropriate photos on your computer.

YOUR WEB HOSTING. To include a photo for free from a third-party web host, you must first upload the photo to your web server, and then enter the address to that photo into the text field here. The address should look something like this: www.yourwebhost.com/ebay/photos/item1.jpg. If everything is correct, the image will be displayed in your auction.

Listing Designer

To help you spice up your auction description, eBay offers the Listing Designer. For an additional 10 cents, this tool allows you to add colorful borders to your listing and select an attractive photo layout. There are quite a few templates from which to choose, so choose carefully and try to find one that is appropriate for the item being auctioned.

Increase your Item's Visibility

eBay provides plenty of options that allow you to set your listing apart from the others. Some are worth the additional cost, some are not.

GALLERY. The Gallery option will display a thumbnail image of your item in search results and listings. Studies show that using this feature increases final sale price by as much as 11 percent. It is well worth the 35 cent price.

SUBTITLE. A subtitle provides a good opportunity to present more information about your item to bidders in search results and category listings. It has not been shown to increase sale price or conversion rate, so judge for yourself whether the extra information this would allow you to display is worth the 50 cents.

BOLD. Selecting the bold option will bold your auction's title in search results and listings. Bolding has been shown to improve final sale price by 7 percent. It costs $1.

BORDER. Adding a border to your listing is a great way to separate it from other auctions. If this option is selected, a colorful thin border will be placed around your auction listing in search results and category lists. Expect this option to boost final sale price by about 7 percent. A border costs $3, and therefore is only worth the expense on high-priced or important promotional auctions.

HIGHLIGHT. At $5, this is the most expensive aesthetic upgrade you can purchase for your listing. Adding a highlight will fill in a colorful background behind your auction listing in search results and category lists. When coupled with a gallery photo, this option really makes your listing stand out. Generally, it increases final sale price by as much as 15 percent.

Promote Your Listing on eBay

For high-priced or important promotional auctions, eBay offers sellers the chance to advertise their auctions in different "featured" locations across the site. These options are expensive, so they are best used sparingly to attract bidders into auctions that will either fetch a high price, or will funnel bidders via cross-promotion into your eBay store and other auctions.

FEATURED PLUS! At the top of search result pages, eBay displays featured auctions above the regular search results. For $19.95 you can place your auction in the featured spot above appropriate search results listings. This option, while expensive, increases the final sale price of your item by a whopping 76 percent. This option also does a great job of funneling bidders into your auction, and into your eBay store.

GALLERY FEATURED. This option is similar to the Featured Plus! option, however, instead of featuring your auction title at the top of all search result and listing pages, this option will display a thumbnail image of your item's first image along with your auction title at the top of the results page when seen in Gallery view. This option is $19.95 and because it is new to eBay, there is no statistical performance information available yet.

HOME PAGE FEATURED. This option is eBay's biggest promotional opportunity. It is quite expensive at $39.95 for one item, and $79.95 for 2 or more items, but it provides the chance for your auction to appear on eBay's main home page—one of the internet's most popular sites. This option increases bidding on your item by 58 percent. Again, this is a great promotional tool when used correctly.

Gift Services

If you would like to suggest that your item would make a nice gift for someone, you can select to place a gift icon next to your listing title for 25 cents. If you choose to advertise your item as a gift, you have the option of advertising the following services: gift wrapping, express shipping, and shipping to a gift recipient instead of the buyer.

Page Counter

A page counter is a basic tool that allows you to see the number of times your auction has been visited. There is no charge to include a counter on your auction page.

Payment Methods

As mentioned earlier, there are several methods for collecting payment from auction winners. If you have registered for a PayPal account, and indicated in your eBay preferences that you would like to accept PayPal payments from buyers, your PayPal information will appear here. If you have chosen to avoid PayPal, you have several options: Money Order/Cashier's Check, Personal Check, and Other/See Item Description. If you select Other/See Item Description you will need to be sure that you state your Other payment terms in your auction's description.

If you have your own merchant account, you can select that you accept Visa/MasterCard, Discover, or American Express through your own terminal.

Ship-To Locations

There are two main options when specifying your shipping terms: Will ship, and Will not ship. If you are interested in only selling to local buyers, and do not require shipping, then you should choose "Will not ship." For all other sellers, you must choose "Will ship . . ." and then select the countries to which you're willing to ship.

Shipping internationally can be risky as much of the fraud that occurs on eBay is perpetrated by people outside the United States—particularly the famous "Nigeria" scam. Some Power-Sellers refuse to ship any items outside the United States to reduce risk of falling victim to scams. Other PowerSellers have no qualms with shipping worldwide. Decide for yourself which best suits you and your business. Though, if you do decide to ship internationally, be cautious. Take extra precaution to make sure that your payment clears, that the address is legitimate, and that all the proper customs forms are filled out accurately.

Shipping and Sales Tax

There are three main options when setting your shipping preferences: flat fee, calculated fees, and freight.

Flat

If you would like to designate a flat shipping rate for all your items to all locations, you can do so in the first shipping tab. You can select up to three different carriers and specify the fees you will charge for each.

Calculated

To more closely estimate what the shipping charges will be for individual bidders, you can choose to use a calculated rate. To do so, you must enter the item's shipping weight and dimensions, and then select up to three carriers. Upon winning an auction, the buyer will insert his or her zip code and the fees will be calculated accordingly. If you are looking to make shipping and handling a profit source, this method will not work for you.

Freight

For large items over 150 pounds, eBay offers freight shipping options. For sellers of toys and hobby items, freight shipping will most likely not be necessary—unless you're sending pallets of steel rocking horses. If you find that you do need freight shipping, simply follow the steps on the freight tab and your auction will be marked accordingly.

Sales Tax

If your state requires you to charge sales tax on internet purchases, you will need to select your state from the pull-down menu and enter the tax rate in the text field. If your state does not require you to charge tax, leave these blank.

Return Policy

If you are planning on accepting returns on items, you will need to check the Returns Accepted box and then fill in the terms under which you will accept returns.

Payment Instructions

If you require special payment instructions, use this field to state them for your bidders. Even if you do not require special payment arrangements, it is a good idea to reiterate your Payment Policies here. You can never be too clear when dealing with your buyers.

Review and Submit

Now that you have configured your auction as you would like, eBay gives you the opportunity to review all the decisions you've made and edit anything that needs fixing. Double check every piece of your auction for accuracy. Spell check your title, description, and shipping and payment policies. It is important that you present everything professionally.

Your auction listing fees will be displayed at the bottom of this page. If everything looks in order, click Submit and begin your auction. If you have not chosen to schedule your auction, it will begin immediately and end after the duration you've chosen expires.

Congratulations, you've submitted your first auction on eBay! Now you get to sit back and watch the bidders bid. Good luck!

eBay Stores

Along with putting merchandise up for auction on eBay, you may want to consider opening an eBay store, which would allow you to sell your fixed price and auction items from a unique destination on eBay. eBay stores make it easy to cross sell your inventory and build repeat business.

According to eBay, you should open an eBay store if you want all your listings displayed in one customizable place; if you want to be able to easily generate repeat business and encourage multiple purchases from the same buyers; if you want to control what you cross-sell to your customers; and if you want to maintain a larger permanent inventory than you can selling through auctions.

eBay stores offer a convenient selling platform for all your eBay listings—auctions, fixed price items, and store inventory. eBay promotes stores in several ways. All your auction listings will contain the eBay store icon; when bidders click on that icon, they are taken to your store. That icon is also attached to your eBay user ID for increased visibility. The eBay store directory is designed to promote all stores and will drive buyers to your particular store. You will also receive your own personalized eBay store web site address that you can distribute and publicize as you wish.

The process of opening an eBay store is almost as simple as setting up your initial user ID. The only requirements are that you be a registered eBay seller and have a minimum feedback rating of 20 or be ID-verified.

Any items that you have in active listings at the time you open your store will not appear in your store. But any auctions or fixed priced listing you post once your store is opened will automatically appear in your eBay store.

The cost of a basic eBay store is a nominal monthly fee (current rates can be found at www.ebay.com) that increases with the level of services you desire, along with additional fees for items listed and sold. Store inventory listings are less expensive than auction listings and appear for a longer time. However, those listings appear only in your store and do not come up in traditional eBay auction searches.

In addition to insertion fees, as with auctions, you also pay final-value fees when an item in a store listing sells.

eBay offers three store levels: basic, featured, and anchor. All have their own customizable storefront and the ability to list store inventory, but featured and anchor stores include additional services. Here's how the three levels differ from one another:

1. *Basic.* Your store is automatically listed in the eBay Stores Directory and will appear in every category directory where you have items listed.

2. *Featured.* Your store rotates through a special featured section on the eBay stores home page; receives priority placement in "related stores" on search and listings pages; and it is featured within the category directory pages where you have items listed. In addition, you receive monthly reports on your sales and marketplace performance.

3. *Anchor.* In addition to the services offered to featured stores, your store can be showcased with your logo within the eBay Stores Directory pages. It will also

receive premium placement in "related stores" on search and listings pages, which means your store will be placed higher on the page than the featured stores.

Check the eBay web site for current store subscription fees.

Setting Up Your Store

You want to apply the same principles to stocking your eBay store as you would a bricks-and-mortar store. eBay allows you to create up to 20 custom categories for your products, similar to aisles in a physical store.

You may decide to use product-based categories or you might use a more flexible system, with categories like "sale items," "bestsellers," and "seasonal." Consider having a category for new items so people who visit your store regularly can quickly see what you've added recently. These custom categories can be changed and updated as often as you wish, which is a significant benefit to a seller whose inventory changes frequently.

Your store site should also clearly explain how you operate. Take advantage of the "Store Policies" page to provide a complete and professional description of your policies and procedures. Use "About My Store" to establish your credentials and provide some history about you and your company. Make sure that each store listing incorporates the same features as a traditional auction with a good title, clear pictures, and adequate description.

Use Your Store to Cross-Sell and Up-Sell

All eBay store subscriptions have the advantage of strategically placing promotion boxes in storefronts on different pages that can highlight featured items, provide special announcements, or be used in a variety of ways to showcase your store.

> Be sure to use your store to list all the items you have in your inventory that complement your active auctions, and be sure to mention your store in all your eBay listings.

You also get cross-promotion tools that help you up-sell by allowing you to control which items your buyers see after they bid on or buy one of your items, or use the checkout function after a transaction has ended. You can choose different items to show on each listing.

The tools work by allowing you to establish "merchandising relationships" for the items you list; this determines which items the buyers will be shown. You determine what goes together by designating relationships for as many or as few items as you'd like. If you don't include cross-merchandise on one of your items, eBay will automatically select related items you are selling to display to your buyers.

Understand the Commitment

Your eBay store is open for business 24/7, whether you're awake or asleep. You need to monitor your store closely, answer questions from shoppers promptly, ship merchandise on schedule and as promised, and deal with any other customer service issues that might arise as soon as possible.

If you go on vacation or are going to be away from your store for any reason, you can either arrange for someone else to monitor the site and take care of your business or you can place your store "on vacation" with eBay for an indefinite period. However, you will continue to be charged the normal store subscription and listing fees.

Pricing

*P*RICING IS A CONTENTIOUS ISSUE AMONG EBAY
PowerSellers. Some swear by setting a low
Starting Price and a high Reserve Price, while others avoid Reserve Prices outright fearing that they sabotage the
auction's final sale price and result in lower profits per item. There
is no right answer, and the method that will work best for you
depends largely on the nature of your target bidders, the popularity
of your auctions, and the retail price of your items.

Pricing Strategies

This chapter will provide you with an introduction to all the different
prices you'll need to set when creating an auction, and the strategies

used by PowerSellers when setting those prices. You will need to tinker with these different strategies to find the ones that produce the highest profits for you.

Starting Price

An auction's Starting Price is the lowest amount that the first bidder will need to bid in order to participate in the auction. Many sellers make the case that this Starting Price should be set to the lowest amount that you're willing to accept for an item while retaining an acceptable profit margin. If your aim is to make a 20 percent profit on everything you sell, then this price should simply be set to 20 percent higher than what it cost you to buy, pack, and ship the item. This method is most near traditional brick-and-mortar pricing methods because it guarantees profitability. But, like traditional brick-and-mortar pricing methods, it does not guarantee sales.

The next pricing methods are more suited to eBay's dynamic and fluid pricing phenomena. Sellers who are willing to gamble their profit margins are more likely to capitalize on the eBay buyer bidding frenzy phenomenon. The aim of this strategy is to create a frenzy around every auction by capitalizing on a bidder's competitive drive to win. This frenzy, when created successfully, drives up the item's final sale price and awards higher profits to the seller. How does one create this frenzy? There are a few ways to do it.

ONE DOLLAR, LOW RESERVE. First is the "$1LR" method, or the "One Dollar, Low Reserve" method. This strategy begins by setting a $1 or lower starting price on an item. The item could be either an old set of jumping jacks, or a vintage Monopoly set worth thousands—the item's real-world value is not taken into account. The low starting price encourages bargain-hunting bidders to jump into the auction early. The increased number of bidders sends your item's price skyward during the auction, whittling out the less enthusiastic bidders as the price goes up. But many of the original bidders will remain, either because they know the $1LR tactic and have expected to pay a fair price for the item from the beginning, or because they are now emotionally invested in the auction and feel compelled to win. Each bid, whether by calculation or compulsion, drives up your item's price.

Listing expensive inventory for $1 would frighten any reasonable businessperson. Therefore, this method includes a safety net in the Low Reserve price set at the auction's outset. This reserve price should be set low enough that bidders do not become discouraged when their bids repeatedly do not surpass the hidden reserve price, yet high enough that you don't lose your profits when the item sells. One of the keys to making this strategy work is that you must advertise that you have set a Low Reserve somewhere in your auction. Every bidder will see that you have set a reserve price, but the amount of that reserve is hidden from them. Reserve prices tend to scare off bidders who are skeptical that sellers are overvaluing their items, and making the reserve prices too near retail prices. Therefore, for this strategy to work, you must set the price low, and advertise that you have done so.

ONE DOLLAR, NO RESERVE. The most controversial pricing method is known as the "$1NR" method, or, as you may have guessed, the "One Dollar, No Reserve" method. This strategy is similar to the above strategy, though it is far riskier in that without setting a reserve price, your rare vintage G.I. Joe dolls might very well sell for a dollar, leaving you with the financial loss. Many sellers use this strategy successfully, trusting that if they have promoted the item well enough, the eBay bidding community will determine the fair market value for the item. And, because the hope of buying a valuable doll for only a few dollars draws in a large number of early bidders, there is a greater chance of a bidding war developing and driving profits through the roof.

"I think $1NR auctions are a good thing. Starting with a low bid price, with no reserve, sparks interest and activity. That's what you want. There will be times when you may not get what you expect, but the traffic and exposure to your other listings is worth it."

—MGMagic

Be cautious when using or experimenting with the $1NR strategy. It often falls victim to sniping, wherein savvy bidders wait until the closing seconds of an auction to place a bid, thereby securing a huge bargain by not allowing time for the item's price to reach fair market value. This method also should not be used alone, as it can prevent the growth of a business by limiting the number of similar items that can be sold at one time—the higher the number of items available will lower the demand for that item, and therefore your final selling price. The $1NR method is best used as a promotional tool to draw bidders into auctions where the seller is cross-promoting their auctions that use not-so-risky pricing strategies.

It should be noted that if you choose to use either the $1LR or $1NR method of pricing, setting your Starting Price at 99 cents instead of one dollar would work just as effectively in drawing in bidders, but would also save you money in listing fees due to eBay's listing fee structure.

Buy It Now

The Buy It Now price caters to convenience buyers who would rather pay your asking price than wait a week for your auction to end. Over 25 percent of the items sold on eBay are sold through stores, BIN, or other fixed-price sales. So, to pass-over setting a BIN price is to pass-over a substantial number of your buyers. It should be used as an important part of your overall pricing strategy.

The first BIN method applies if you have opted for a conservative pricing strategy and set your Starting Prices at a

> "We have no problem with people starting their auctions at one dollar. However, we try to stay away from that type of starting price due to the already small profit margin on the items we sell. We normally try to start an item at a price which may not necessarily be what we ultimately want for an item, but would at least allow us to break even if the item only sells for the starting price."
>
> —mrandjr

level that would produce a profit. By setting your BIN price slightly higher than your Starting Price, you can encourage bidders to bypass the lengthy bidding process and purchase the item immediately. It may be worth the few extra dollars to them to skip the days of watching and bidding. This method works well with relatively inexpensive items that are not likely to create a bidding frenzy, or with items that are in high demand and you are confident that you will receive your asking price.

The second BIN method is used in conjunction with the $1NR promotional strategy. By setting a BIN price within a $1NR auction, you are achieving two things: attracting a high number of potential convenience buyers, and planting a suggestion in the minds of the bidders as to what is a fair price for the item at auction. eBay buyers are smart and often do research, both on eBay and off, to find the fair market value for the item you are selling. But that doesn't mean that setting a BIN price for them to bid toward will not affect bidding habits.

Reserve Price

There is little strategy behind setting a Reserve Price. Bidders tend to opt for auctions without a set Reserve Price due to the promise of a better bargain, and therefore they should be used sparingly. Though, if you are testing a new item to see what kind of bids it produces, or cannot bear to see it sell for less than a certain amount, then a Reserve Price is a good idea. PowerSellers rarely use Reserves, and in some cases, when they do opt to use a Reserve Price, they go so far as to state what the reserve price is in the item's description. This provides the seller with a price guarantee, and the bidder with the knowledge of how much they would need to pony up. This method is unconventional and rarely used as setting your Starting Price would produce the same effective result, but it is worth consideration.

Profitability versus Risk

Finding an effective pricing strategy is an exercise in balancing profitability and risk. A high-risk strategy may yield a few highly profitable sales, but it will not do so reliably. A conservative strategy can make sure that every sale you make is reliably profitable, but sales could be slow or yield small profits.

The most effective pricing plan makes use of a combination of these strategies. High-risk strategies are effective in attracting the attention of bidders. Use cross promotion within those high-risk auctions as promotional tools for your low-risk auctions, fixed-price items, and store. Soon, your high-risk auctions will be leading bidders into your other more reliably profitable sales channels within eBay.

Selling
Your Items

*N*OW THAT YOU'RE FAMILIAR WITH THE LOGISTICS OF starting an auction on eBay, it is time for some fine-tuning. To receive the highest price for your items you will need to put some thought and care into your item's auction. There are three main areas: the title, the description, and the photos.

The importance of creating quality titles, descriptions, and photos in your auctions cannot be understated. This is your opportunity to communicate directly to buyers. With the competition as fierce as it is in the Toys & Hobbies category, you must communicate effectively.

The Title

The auction title has two important jobs. First, it provides the keywords that eBay uses to produce results when buyers use the site's search function. Most buyers find their items through eBay's search function, and while it is possible for buyers to search both title and description, the site's default setting searches only auction titles. So be sure when writing your title that you use any keywords that a buyer might use when searching for your item. Remember, the title has a limit of 55 characters.

Here are some things to keep in mind when writing your titles.

Always include, if available:

- Manufacturer's name
- Model number
- Series name
- Item condition
- Pertinent information (color, animal type, complete set, etc.)

Avoid:

- Space-wasting attention grabbers (L@@K!!)
- ALL CAPS
- Unconventional abbreviations
- Adjectives (Use these in your description)

Here are two titles for the same Monopoly game.

Good Title
1970s Franklin Mint Collectors Monopoly Edition, NIB

Bad Title

AWESOME!!! Very Old Monopoly Board Game GR8!

The first title is packed with information to help the buyer know exactly what is up for auction. It contains keywords that a buyer would use to search for such a Monopoly edition, and all of the abbreviations used are industry standards that buyers seeking this item would know. "NIB" means "New In Box" and is a standard eBay abbreviation. The second title may catch the bidder's eye more readily among the other titles on the page, but it contains few keywords and wastes space with exclamation points, useless adjectives, and by spelling out words that can be abbreviated. Not only would this second title not come up in searches, it gives the bidder no indication of what they will see if they look at this auction. The bidder will not waste time with this listing and move on.

Description

Investing time in writing a good description will pay off in the price you receive. Your description should include:

- the name of the item;
- what the item is made of;
- when and where it was made;
- who made it (company, artist, designer, author, etc.);
- what condition it's in;
- weight, size, and/or dimensions;
- notable features or markings;
- and any special background or history.

Maintain a database of pictures so its easy to pull up images for listings when you are selling items you've sold before.

When photographing toy boxes with any kind of clear plastic front, be careful that the glare from the camera's flash doesn't wash out the image and obscure the item you're displaying. Show all your items from various angles. Help the bidder see exactly what he would be looking for if it were in his or her hands.

Invest in a digital camera. You don't have to get the top-of-the-line model, but get a camera that has more than two megapixels and a macro function for clear close-up detail shots. Your customers will want to see the intricacies of train sets, the stitching on plush toys, the scratches on any model cars, the pieces of a board game, and so on. Therefore, a macro function for clarity is important.

If you have a scanner, you can use print film and then scan your photos. However, this process is time consuming and costly. If you plan to sell on eBay with any regularity, invest in a digital camera. Once you have the pictures uploaded to your computer you can then use a program to adjust and enhance your images. Be sure that all the parts of the image are bright and clear.

Copyrights

When writing your descriptions and uploading your photos, be sure that you are using original content. The practice of cutting and pasting item descriptions from a manufacturer's web site is common because it makes quick work of providing accurate information; however, this practice can be dangerous as some manufacturers copyright the promotional materials for their products. If you choose to use text or photos from an outside source in your auction listings, be sure that it is not copyrighted material. If you see no copyright symbol, don't assume that it is free to use. Contact the company and ask for permission to use their photos or text. Most manufacturers are happy to give you permission. Though it only takes one disgruntled corporate lawyer to ruin your day. When in doubt, it is best to create original content.

"I have a Nikon Coolpix 3200. I use it on the lowest resolution, which is more than enough for pictures on a computer screen, and give buyers clear enough details of the item they're buying. I see a lot of people buying five, six, even eight megapixel cameras and spending hundreds of dollars on wasted technology. My camera is only three megapixels and I never need the higher settings."

—toysheik

CHAPTER 8

Customer
Care

*E*VEN BEFORE YOU SUBMIT YOUR AUCTION TO EBAY, you must be thinking about customer care. eBay bidders are sophisticated people, and care every bit as much about the way they are treated as the real-world retail shopper. This proper treatment begins when you are putting together your item's auction page.

Pre-Auction

Bidders expect your auction page to be professional, attractive, error-free, and easy to use. If your page has typos, incorrect information, fuzzy photos, or just plain old hard-to-read bricks of text, bidders will shop somewhere else. Take extra care to consider your bidders when formatting and writing your auction pages. Be sure to invite bidders to contact you with questions. In addition to eBay's "Ask seller a question" link, provide an e-mail address and phone number where you can be reached with questions. Make it as easy as possible for bidders to do business with you.

When writing your description, try to anticipate questions bidders might ask you. Answer any hypothetical questions you can think of. Taking some extra time when writing your descriptions will save you loads of time in answering e-mails and phone calls.

During Auctions

During auctions you will need to be available to your customers in case a few of them need to ask you questions. As any PowerSeller will tell you, answering questions from bidders will quickly become a lot of work.

Questions

Answering questions from bidders can become a tiresome and frustrating task. There will be nights when you are tired; it is 2 A.M., and you've got 50 more questions to answer. It is during these times that you must keep your feedback score in mind. Be polite and professional in your answers. If you are receiving the same question over and over again, write a polite and thorough answer once and then cut and paste it to the 20 people who need it. If the question comes to you through the eBay message center, it will be posted on the auction's page for future questioners to see. The more patient you are with your customers, the more loyal they will be to you in the future.

There may come a point when you will need to hire someone to help you slog through all the questions. When selling specialty items, such as collectibles, you will receive more questions than most sellers. People don't bother so much about specifics when buying textbooks or old monitors off eBay. But, when it comes to building collections, bidders will need to know every last detail about our product. Make sure when you hire someone to help you answer questions that he or she is as knowledgeable about your products are you are.

Post-Auction

Once an auction ends, be sure to contact the winner right away to congratulate him or her and present the next steps. Constant and clear communication will help the transaction occur smoothly. As soon after the end of the auction as you can, send an invoice with the item number, the auction's total price, and instructions for submitting payment to you. Be sure to thank the winner for his or her business and to give the e-mail a personal tone. For a nominal fee, eBay will automate this for you. Many PowerSellers take advantage of this option, but caution new sellers to make sure that the e-mail does not sound automated. Customers would rather deal with a person than a machine, even though sometimes it just isn't feasible for sellers.

After the winning bidder has submitted payment, they will expect a receipt and quick shipment of their item. Many PowerSellers, when they do receive negative feedback, receive it because the bidder was disappointed with the speed of shipping. If you cannot ship an item immediately for some reason, be sure that you contact the buyer and make him aware of the delay. If you know about a possible delay prior to posting an auction, mention it in the auction's description. It is better to be honest than disappointing.

Once the payment has been received and the package has been shipped, e-mail the bidder to let him know that his item is on the way. If you have shipped via a carrier that uses a tracking number, include that in the e-mail so that the bidder can watch anxiously as it approaches his house.

Then, once the transaction is complete, provide timely positive feedback if warranted. If you've done everything right, you will be rewarded with positive feedback in return. Remember, although you cannot make everyone happy, as evidenced by the overwhelmingly positive feedback ratings of some PowerSellers, it is possible to come pretty darn close.

When Things Go Wrong

Sometimes you will make mistakes. For the most part, buyers are understanding people and will be forgiving if you are straightforward with them. When mistakes happen, do what you need to do to make things right for the customer. Remember, because this is your business, you have the power and authority to do what needs to be done. Don't hesitate to offer a partial or full refund if it means keeping a customer.

If you run into a belligerent customer who cannot be reasoned with, remain calm. You may receive quite unpleasant e-mails or worse from angry customers, but you must not allow it to affect how you deal with the problem. Read the customer's entire e-mail, apologize for the problem, ask her how you can best solve the dilemma, and then thank her for her patience and understanding—even if she showed you none. You will be surprised how many irate customers can be turned into grateful customers with a polite and apologetic e-mail.

Beware of Scams

One of the most well-known scams on eBay occurs when a winning bidder receives an item from the seller and immediately contacts the seller with a complaint of some sort. Most times the buyer will complain of damage during shipping, misstated condition of the item, or an incorrect shipment. The buyer will then demand a full or partial refund and threaten to post negative feedback to the seller if he does not comply. As seller, it would seem that you have two poor options: comply or take the negative feedback. But that is not the case. If you deem the item worth the cost of attempting recovery, you have a third option. In your best pleasant and understanding tone, apologize for the damage/mistake and offer either an exchange if you have an identical item in stock, or a full refund upon receipt of the damaged or incorrect item. In this scenario you may need to cough up the return shipping charges, but at least you're not losing the value of the item or being scammed out of honestly earned revenue.

Conflict Resolution

eBay will rarely provide aid in a conflict between a buyer and seller. You are pretty much on your own to settle conflicts professionally. However, eBay will come to your aid in certain circumstances. Here are a few:

- eBay receives a court order finding that feedback you've received is slanderous or illegal in some way.
- feedback you've received has obscene, racist, or vulgar language.
- feedback you've received reveals your personal information, such as your home address.
- buyer has bid on your items for the sole purpose of leaving negative feedback.

In these instances you are encouraged to contact eBay for their help. In most other instances, you're left to your own devices.

Don't Fight Fire with Fire

Sellers have the ability to respond to negative feedback that they feel is unwarranted. If you choose to respond to negative feedback you have received, and you should, don't use it as a way to fight back. Remain calm and stick to the facts of the matter. For example, if you get burned with negative feedback for late shipping, but you stated clearly in your auction that shipping would be delayed for this item, simply make a note of that underneath the negative feedback. For example:

Neg: *Seller waited five days before shipping out my Lego set!*

Reply: *Delayed ship date was clearly stated in item description for duration of auction.*

Try to remain calm, factual, and emotionless. The potential bidders who read your feedback comments will appreciate your cool-headed professionalism.

CHAPTER 9

Starting
a Business

STARTING ANY BUSINESS, WHETHER IT IS BASED ON eBay or not, requires careful planning. Before you invest the family savings in a thousand Erector Sets or cap guns, you should sit down and think through your upcoming adventure. There are many things to consider. In this chapter, we'll cover the most important things to think about, and then provide you with some places to find help when you need it.

Finances

There are two ways to go about building your business financially. You can start small, using some extra personal funds to buy inventory, and then slowly build your inventory and subsequent sales as you begin collecting profits. Or, you could seek out a bank loan to help you stock your shelves and begin your business with more sales and faster turnover.

Building your business slowly is the safer option financially because of the low start-up costs, although it requires time, patience, and a lot of work in addition to your day job. This method also gives your larger competition the ability to beat you on price. When you are first starting out, you'll need to buy from your item sources in small quantities, which is often more expensive per item than buying in large quantities. Larger sellers who are able to buy large quantities for the discounts are then able to offer their items at lower prices. Their higher sales volume will also produce more revenue (and profits) for them per month, making it even easier for them to buy in large quantities.

The main benefit to starting slowly is that you'll be free of debt. Starting a business without a loan gives you the freedom to grow at your own pace, take time off if necessary, and even pull the plug if you decide that selling on eBay isn't for you.

Taking out a loan could make your start-up easier. You will be able to buy inventory in larger quantities, sell more items for lower prices, making competing with other sellers easier right off the bat. Getting the loan itself will be challenging because banks do not pass out money to start-ups. In fact, most banks will not provide your business with a loan unless you have already established reliable item sources, a solid customer base, and a track record of profits that proves your business's ability to make payments on the loan. These requirements sometimes make it hard for start-ups to find financing. But there are options.

If you feel confident in your business, you might consider taking out a personal loan or a second mortgage on your home. This is considerably more risky than a business loan because if your business fails you stand to lose your house and income in one blow. Also, because it is a personal loan, you will still owe the bank long after the business is gone. So, if you decide to take this route, be sure that you have done all the planning and anticipation that you can, right down to the smallest detail. Here are some things to consider.

Business Type

For tax purposes you will need to define your business to the Internal Revenue Service (IRS). There are several types of business classifications to choose from, each with benefits and drawbacks. Choose the one that best suits your intentions.

Sole Proprietorship

A sole proprietorship is the most common type of start-up business because it requires little paperwork. You are the only owner. Legally, financially, and tax-wise there is no difference between you and your business. Your business's assets are your assets. Your business's debt is your personal debt. And your business's profits are your income.

The advantage to this type of business is that it is easy to start and you keep all the profits for yourself. You need only to file a business income form (Schedule C) along with your regular taxes. The disadvantage of this type of business is that you are personally liable for all the business debt and mistakes. If your business is sued for any reason, you are directly sued.

Partnership

A partnership is similar to a sole-proprietorship, except instead of one proprietor, there are two. Both parties are legally and financially responsible for the business. Some partnerships are based on common interests (such as husband-wife teams) and some are based on financial need (such as the financier and the manager).

If you're interested in setting up a partnership, be sure to be excruciatingly clear going in to the business about who takes on what role, who makes what decisions, and who receives what money. A clearly defined relationship will go a long way toward making the business relationship a success.

Corporation

Unlike a sole proprietorship or partnership, a corporation is its own legal entity. A corporation's debt, taxes, profits, and legal liability are separate from the corporate owner. While this provides immense protection for owners, corporations can be tricky and expensive to get started, and is therefore not often the first choice of start-up businesses. If you're interested in starting a corporation, you should contact an attorney in your area for help.

S Corporations

An S corporation provides tax benefits to owners. Instead of taxing owners twice like corporations do, once as corporate income tax and once on owner dividends, an S corporation doesn't pay taxes on its corporate income. Owners only pay taxes on their own income from the S corporation.

S corporations also offer all the same legal and financial protections that corporations do, so this may be a smarter choice for your start-up.

Limited Liability Corporation

Like an S corporation, Limited Liability Corporations (LLCs) provide owners with legal and financial protection while avoiding the double taxation that occurs in corporations. This is quickly becoming the default choice for small businesses. Setting up an LLC is relatively easy as well. Talk to your local chamber of commerce or SCORE chapter about where to find the necessary forms.

Registering your Business Name

In many states it is necessary for you to register your business name, sometimes called a "fictitious name," with the state before you can do such things as open a business bank account or apply for a bank loan. Registering your business name also ensures that you have the rights to that name in your state. Other companies will still be able to operate under your registered name, but if it ever came to a legal battle, you would have claim. Registration is a simple process that involves a simple form, a small processing fee, and a stamp. Check with your state's Small Business Association web site for more information.

Inventory Issues

Buying your inventory can be seen as the "no-turning-back" point. Once you've made such a large investment, you're pretty well committed to making the business work. That's why it is very important to take care of your inventory as closely as you would if it were the actual cash equivalent.

Storage

Your inventory must be stored safely in an appropriate facility. A lot of the items you'll be dealing in require a dry and clean storage area. Plush toys can quickly collect mold. Card games can grow soggy. Even die-cast vehicles can begin to rust after a while. Cardboard boxes must be kept up off the concrete floor to prevent moisture damage. Your inventory must also be stored in a manner that makes it easy to retrieve the items you need without moving a bunch of boxes around to get to them. Continuously moving boxes of fragile equipment will, over time, destroy your inventory.

Many PowerSellers who start their businesses in their basements quickly realize that the damp, dark, soggy conditions are less than ideal for their needs. Before long these sellers were able to rent storage facilities in the less-expensive industrial areas around their towns. The low rents and large facilities suit their businesses perfectly. They have plenty of space to store their inventories, plenty of room for their shipping departments, and plenty of room for the FedEx or UPS trucks to back up to the loading docks. A fancy and expensive Main Street storefront is not required as all of their selling occurs online.

Before you make the investment in inventory, be sure that you have arranged for the proper facilities to receive, manage, store, and ship that inventory.

Materials

Besides investing in your inventory, you will also need to make an investment in supplies for your business. You will obviously need a computer, though a computer capable of loading eBay can be found quite inexpensively these days. You will also need shipping materials that are appropriate for the items you will be shipping. As the seller, it is your responsibility to make sure that your item is packed in such a way that it can withstand a reasonable amount of abuse while in transit.

You can find all these items on eBay. Savvy sellers have realized that one of the largest markets on eBay is, in fact, other sellers; therefore packing and shipping materials are quite easy to find at great prices all over eBay. If you're in a rush and don't want to wait a few days for delivery, try your local Staples, Office Depot, UPS Store, or U-Haul supply store. They all generally have adequate packing and shipping departments.

CHAPTER 10

Tools to Help
You Work Smarter

*A*N INDUSTRY IS GROWING TO AID EBAY SELLERS. Research, software, and consulting companies are being created every day to help sellers sell. As a result, many tools are available to make selling easier, faster, and most cost efficient. Even eBay itself provides many tools to help you along. In this chapter, we'll cover some of eBay's tools and some of the third-party solutions that are available to help you reach PowerSeller status.

To help sellers discover even more helpful tools, eBay has created a directory full of third-party solutions. Visit the directory by clicking the Solutions Directory link on the left side of eBay's main page.

Research Tools

Choosing the correct items to sell is a key factor to your business's success. To help you make an informed decision, companies have released the following research tools. Be sure to take advantage of at least one of these services before you begin selling in earnest.

eBay Pulse

eBay Pulse, at http://pulse.ebay.com, will provide you with some general information about the current popular trends in eBay buying and selling. Choose Toys & Hobbies from the pull-down menu to find the latest trends in the category. This simple page will tell you the most popular toy category searches, the largest toy stores, and the most watched toys and hobby items. This information changes every day, and is therefore a good thing to keep an eye on. Click through the top searches to find top-selling items for that particular search term. Is there anything in there that you might like to sell? Who is selling the most of these items? Can you find ways to do it better? Browse through the largest stores to find out what they've got to offer. eBay Pulse is a great place to begin thinking about what the hot items are in the Toys & Hobbies category, and what you would like to begin selling.

Marketplace Research

eBay also offers a service called Marketplace Research. This tool provides a place for sellers to do more in depth research about the items they are, or hope to begin, selling. Sellers can find up to 90 days of completed listing information, as opposed to the usual 30 days available through Advanced Search; top searches in a particular category or across the whole site; average sale and average start price for any given item; and many other tools.

There are three subscription levels: Fast Pass, Basic, and Pro. Fast Pass is a nonrenewing two-day subscription for $2.99. Basic and Pro are monthly subscriptions that can be had for $9.99 and $24.99 respectively. You can view the details of Marketplace Research and the services offered to the different subscription levels at http://pages.ebay.com/marketplace_research.

This service receives mixed reviews from sellers. Some complain that it is overpriced and is limited in its services, whereas many others applaud the service as being helpful and thorough. Visit the Marketplace Research discussion board to read some reviews before taking the plunge. In our experience it has been quite helpful for quick research, though limited in its offerings compared to the more established eBay research companies.

Terapeak.com

Terapeak.com's Marketplace Research tool is similar to eBay's Marketplace Research tool in that it allows you to research market trends, item performance, buyer habits, and more for any given item or category. Terapeak is well regarded as an easy-to-use and effective service that has been helping eBay sellers since 2003. It is an online tool and requires no software download. The service has two subscription levels: Research Lite for $9.95 per month, or Research Complete for $16.95 per month or $169.50 per year.

Andale

Andale is the most well-known eBay market research company. They have been around almost since the inception of eBay itself. Their research tool is called, appropriately, Andale Research. It is a web-based tool, thereby avoiding the problems of operating-system-specific programs, and is the lowest priced at only $7.95 per month.

Andale Research can tell you much of the same information as the services above, such as item and category information. But it will also provide you with a recommendation for what time of the day and week to list your item for maximum profitability; a comparison of an item's eBay selling price compared to retail selling prices on Froogle, Shopping.com, and BizRate. It will also tell you which type of listing (auction, Buy It Now, etc.) will get you the best price for your item.

In addition to the market research tools, Andale offers a whole line of services to help the eBay seller, such as Sales Analyzer to help you get maximum profit from your existing listings, and Andale Supplier, a tool to help you find the best source for the items you sell. Find out more at www.andale.com.

HammerTap's DeepAnalysis 2

HammerTap offers quite a few services to help the eBay seller. Their market research tool, DeepAnalysis 2, is a software download. It helps sellers find out what is selling by analyzing data and providing reports about specific eBay sellers, categories, items, and keywords. DeepAnalysis 2 not only helps sellers find out what is selling, but also why. It finds the average starting price, auction length, and the payment types accepted for items that are selling the most reliably. You can use this information to fine tune your own listings for better sales. DeepAnalysis 2 is a robust tool with many ways to help a seller, only a fraction of which we're able to cover here. It does, however, have some drawbacks. It is fairly expensive at $17.95 per month, and runs only on Windows, leaving out Mac and Linux users. Take advantage of the free trial, judge for yourself. See www.hammertap.com.

Auction Management Tools

Submitting every auction via eBay's web site would be clunky, time-consuming, and visually painful. PowerSellers could not have become PowerSellers if they spent all their time listing individual auctions through eBay's web site. Therefore, to facilitate listing more than a few products per month, many companies have created software that helps sellers list, duplicate, re-list, and manage their auctions. A few that are commonly used by PowerSellers are listed in the following sections.

eBay's Tools

eBay provides a few tools to help sellers better manage their auctions. They include:

- *TurboLister.* A bulk listing tool with HTML Templates.
- *Selling Manager.* An online auction management tool that includes feedback templates, bulk relisting, invoicing, downloadable sales history, and bulk feedback. Best when used in conjunction with TurboLister.
- *Selling Manager Pro.* An online auction management tool that includes inventory management, listing statistics, bulk feedback and invoicing, automated e-mails, and more.
- *Seller's Assistant Basic.* A download application for PCs that helps sellers create listings, manage auctions, and manage customer correspondence.
- *Seller's Assistant Pro.* A download application for PCs that is a complete auction management tool. It creates listings, manages auctions, manages customer correspondence, handles bulk processing, and helps with post-auction tasks, such as invoicing.

Auctiva

Auctiva is a free tool that helps sellers create listings, schedule auctions, cross-market auctions, host images, manage sales, generate reports, and increase efficiency. It is an online tool. To learn more, or to sign up, visit www.auctiva.com.

ChannelAdvisor

ChannelAdvisor offers all levels of service from helping you manage your first few auctions, to helping large corporations liquidate entire companies. Their auction management software is ChannelAdvisor Pro. It is a web-based tool that offers templates for your listings, image hosting, inventory management capabilities, customer correspondence, and post-auction checkout. One of the benefits of ChannelAdvisor is the many levels of service they provide. You will not outgrow their services. For more information, visit www.channel advisor.com.

> "I recently received a shipment of new toys and an old Star Wars collection on the day before I had to fly to Ireland for a trip. Because I had TurboLister installed on my laptop, I was able to do it in Ireland while enjoying a nice cold pint of Guinness. I'm telling you it just doesn't get any better than that."
>
> —toysheik

Photo Hosting Services

To become a PowerSeller you will need to display as many photos of your items as you can. Research shows that there is direct relationship between the number of photos in an auction and the final sale price. Simply put, buyers want to see what they're buying, and the more you can show to them, the more likely they are to make the purchase. If you stick with eBay's photo services, adding more photos means adding to the listing price, and when you are listing several thousand items a month, a difference of 45 cents per item will add up fast. To avoid those per-photo fees, you can use one of these photo hosting services listed in the following sections and then link to the photos in your auctions description with a simple HTML tag. Your auction will be able to display as many photos you like at no incremental cost.

FotoTime

For only $23.95 per year, FotoTime provides enough storage for you to have thousands of photos online. They also provide thumbnail versions of each photo you upload for convenient placement into your auction pages. For more information, go to www.fototime.com.

VillagePhotos

VillagePhoto has many different photo hosting plans for you to choose from. They offer low prices and useful options such as a browser uploading tool, a photo album from easy management, and automatic thumbnails. If you plan to grow beyond eBay into other online marketplaces, VillagePhotos also integrates well with Yahoo! Auctions and Yahoo! Stores.

Their plans start at just $3.95 per month. For more information, visit www.villagephotos.com.

Photobucket.com

Photobucket.com is a free online photo hosting and album service. They have an online uploading tool, photo manager, a public photo album feature, and easy eBay integration. They also integrate well with other web sites such as my space.com and other blog sites.

These are just some of the tools that help sellers. If you can't find what you need here, visit eBay's Solution Directory for hundreds of more programs. Also, you can visit www.auction softwarereview.com for an independent source of auction management software downloads and reviews.

"I use a workflow automation program called Shooting Star from Foo Dog Software. It helps me track new sales, pending payments, and shipping status. The best feature is its customer notification options. I can keep my customers in the loop from start to finish. They know exactly when I received their payment and when I've shipped their item. I can't say enough about this invaluable tool."

—MGMagic

CHAPTER 11

Advanced
Marketing Strategies

$\int$ INCE ITS LAUNCH IN 1995, EBAY HAS GROWN TO become exactly what it touts itself to be: The World's Online Marketplace. In the early days, marketing was not much of a concern for sellers, simply listing items for auction was enough. But today, due to the astronomical growth in the number of auctions running at any given time, losing your auctions in the crowd is a distinct possibility. Today, marketing is a must. If you are not taking steps to attract large numbers of bidders to your auctions, they will be overshadowed. Your sales rates will suffer along with your final sale price. Fortunately, there are relatively simple steps you can take to ensure that interested buyers find your auction. Some of the strategies employed by PowerSellers are outlined in this chapter.

Marketing within eBay

Within the eBay structure, there are many ways to market your items. Timing plays a key role, as does a teaser auction, using featured listings, keywords, e-mail marketing, and correspondence promotion.

Timing Your Auctions

An auction is most visible when it is in its final few minutes. eBay's listing sort order defaults to "Time: ending soonest," and therefore the auctions with the least time left rise to the top of the page. Most buyers never bother to resort the listing to anything other than the default, and therefore the overwhelming majority of bidders who see your auction see it in its final few minutes. So, naturally, you benefit by aligning those final few minutes of your auction with eBay's peak traffic times. This makes the time when your auction is most visible also the time when there are the most bidders on eBay.

The conventional wisdom, as mentioned in Chapter 5, is that Sunday nights between the hours of 6 P.M. and midnight (EST) are eBay's peak traffic hours. In our own research we found that over 50 percent of PowerSellers asked claimed Sunday to be the most successful day to end an auction. Monday was a distant second with only 10 percent of the vote.

There are two ways to end an auction during peak hours. You could manually submit your auction during that time and set the auction's duration for seven days. Though, if you have more than a few auctions to submit, this process will be time consuming and slow given the high traffic on eBay's site during this time. Or, you could simply pay eBay the additional 10 cents per listing and schedule your auctions to begin during this time slot with a seven day duration. Also, some of the auction management software outlined in Chapter 10 allows you to schedule listings. There are fees associated with doing it via these programs as well, though the more expensive ones integrate the scheduling costs into your monthly fee.

Teaser Auctions

Now that you've got your auctions timed to maximize exposure, you can begin guiding traffic into your auctions, fixed-price listings, and eBay store with teaser auctions. A teaser auction is set up just like a regular auction, but using a highly popular item, a low starting price, and Cross-Promotion. The Cross-Promotion tool is available to eBay store owners and places thumbnails of items you've selected from your store into all of your auctions, thereby advertising your more profitable items to interested bidders. These teaser auctions are designed to show up in the main site's search results listings to capture the attention of bidders traveling eBay's main traffic stream.

Featured Listings

When you can afford to, take advantage of eBay's Featured Listings promotional tools. These are expensive, but when used with your eBay store and the Cross-Promotion tool, are highly effective at driving a lot of bidders to your store and auctions. Always use your best-selling items in these featured auctions, and make sure that the products you've chosen to cross-promote are directly related to the featured auction's item. Bidders will not follow a link to an item for which they have no interest. Also, as these will be your most prominent auctions, be sure to spellcheck your text, proofread, and double check your photos for clarity and accuracy. It is important that these highly visible auctions reflect your business well.

eBay Keywords

The eBay Keywords program is an effective and performance-based method of promoting your items within eBay. Like other keyword purchasing programs from top search engines like Google and Yahoo!, eBay auctions off search keywords to interested sellers. The winning bid is the highest offered price-per-click rate. The winning bidders are awarded the opportunity to display a banner advertisement at the top of the eBay search results page for that keyword. Every time a customer clicks on the seller's banner advertisement, they pay eBay the price-per-click rate that was offered during bidding.

For example, say a seller, Caroline, had an eBay store stocked full of new and vintage LiteBrites from Hasbro. If she were to participate in the eBay Keywords program, she would do well to submit the highest bid for the term "litebrite." When a customer submitted a search using the term "litebrite," Caroline's banner advertisement showcasing her LiteBrites would be displayed above all the other thousands of regular results. Only when a customer clicks on Caroline's banner advertisement does she pay eBay for the use of that spot. Caroline might also consider bidding on common misspellings of LiteBrite, such as LightBright, LiteBright, and so on. These misspellings could provide some decent traffic and come at a lower price.

The eBay Keywords program can lead a lot of bidders into your store or auctions in a short amount of time. It is one of the best return-on-investments in eBay promotion. For more information, go to www.ebaykeywords.com.

E-Mail Marketing

Included in your eBay store subscription is an E-Mail Marketing tool that allows your customers to subscribe to your eBay store newsletter. An e-mail newsletter can be a great way to promote sales, specials, your store, and your auctions. The E-Mail Marketing tool lets you manage up to five e-mail lists so you can customize your newsletters to your buyers' specific interests.

By doing business on eBay you will be in constant contact with your customers via e-mail. Even if you choose not to use your eBay store E-Mail Marketing tool, it would be a good idea to begin building a database of the e-mail addresses of your customers. Keep careful notes about what each person has purchased from you for appropriate sorting later.

As mentioned earlier, eBay has a strict no-spamming rule that you need to adhere to when putting together e-mail campaigns. You must ask your customers if they would like to subscribe to your mailing list before you begin sending out e-mails, and provide them with a way to opt out later if they accept. If you use your eBay Store's E-Mail Marketing tool, this will be taken care of for you. If you plan to collect and market to e-mail addresses on your own, get permission first.

Correspondence Promotion

Every time you have contact with a customer, you are presented with an opportunity to do a little promotion. In every package you ship, insert a flyer advertising an upcoming sale or new product line. On every invoice you print, include the address to your eBay store or make a note about the other popular items you sell. In every e-mail you send out, whether it is a winner confirmation, a payment request, or a post-auction follow-up, include a link to your eBay store. These simple steps are inexpensive, but will help you spread the word about your business in big ways. Always be looking for new promotional ideas.

Marketing Off eBay

It is also wise to promote your products out of the eBay realm. One method is to use your own web site to generate interest. Other ideas are promotional programs and traditional advertising,

Your Own Web Site

Many successful PowerSellers have their own web sites. Some use their sites as complete e-commerce sites separate from eBay, but most find that juggling inventories for two sites is more trouble than it is worth. Your own web site, whether you choose to sell items from it or not, can be a valuable promotional tool for your eBay auctions and store.

> "I don't sell items outside of eBay at the current time. Though I have an external web site that I use to promote my eBay items."
>
> —MGMagic
>
> MGMagic's external web site is at www.mgmagic.com. It displays his current items for sale on eBay. Visit his site for a good example of how your own web site can promote your eBay business.

Searches in the major search engines, such as Google and Yahoo!, will not often produce results from within eBay. Therefore your eBay store, your auctions, and products cannot be easily found through major search engines. This is a large problem, that is, luckily, easily corrected. With a simple independent web site that advertises your eBay store, you can open up your business to the millions of search engine users that would otherwise never see your business. And, by sending customers directly from search engines, to your web site, to your eBay store, you can cleverly route them

> "I don't sell anywhere other than eBay. As a matter of fact, I have even discontinued sales at my own web site, www.toysheik.com. It was very difficult to manage inventory on both eBay and my own web site. For now, my web site is used to store photos, display price guides to the items I sell, and act as a portal to my eBay store."
>
> —toysheik

right past all your eBay competition.

Promotional Programs

Once you have your own web site, you will be able to take advantage of off-eBay promotional services such as Google's AdWords program and Overture's marketing tools. These can significantly increase traffic to your web site and to your eBay auctions and store.

As an additional bonus, eBay recognizes that any off-eBay promotion of your store also promotes eBay as a whole. Therefore, they offer sellers who market their stores off-eBay a 75 percent Final Value Fees discount through the Stores Referral Credit program. See the eBay Stores tutorial pages for more information.

Traditional Real-World Advertising

Don't underestimate the power of traditional, real-world advertising strategies. When used in combination with your own independent web site, placing advertisements in toy and hobbyist trade magazines, on public transportation, and in local newspapers can be quite effective. Advertise your products and your web address just as you would for any other "real" business, because, after all, you have a real business. You'll be attracting market segments that most eBay sellers, and internet businesses in general, rarely think to reach out to.

CHAPTER 12

Inventory
Management

*T*HERE ARE TWO WAYS TO HANDLE THE ITEMS YOU SELL on eBay. You can purchase the items outright and stock them in your warehouse or storage facility yourself, or you can avoid handling inventory all together by finding sources that offer drop-shipping. In this chapter, we'll cover the benefits of both methods so that you can decide which is best for you before you get started.

Drop-Shipping

Drop-shipping is a shipping option that some manufacturers, retailers, and distributors offer to resellers to streamline the selling process. Resellers that use drop-shipping never touch their products. Instead, they simply notify the shipping department at the item's source company when an item is purchased and the item is shipped directly from the source to the customer. This leaves the reseller free to deal with marketing, auction management, customer service, and payment collection without having to set up inventory management or a shipping department.

While drop-shipping may sound like the ideal shipping solution for eBay sellers, it does have significant drawbacks. First and foremost, surrendering control over the shipping of the items you sell puts you entirely at the mercy of the source company. If they run out of stock, or are delayed in shipping, or even fail to ship an item, it will be quite a difficult process for you to get things straightened out with them and then make things right with your customer.

Second, the number of companies that offer drop-shipping is limited; therefore, your options of what to sell are limited. Your decision about what items to sell should be based on profitability and popularity, not on available shipping options.

Finally, if your product line consists of items from only one or two sources and both sources offer drop-shipping, then it might not be a bad idea for you to take advantage of it. However, if you seek to expand your product line in the future, you could end up trying to manage drop-shipments from ten or more companies. This can grow to become so unwieldy and unmanageable that the thought of centralizing all your products and shipments in your own single warehouse may begin to appeal to you.

Taking on Inventory

If you've made the decision that drop-shipping isn't your cup of tea, then you've got some planning ahead of you. The first step is finding the finances to make the initial investment in inventory. The second step is finding a storage or warehouse location that meets your needs. And finally, you will need to put together a comprehensive strategy for taking care of all your new goodies.

Proper inventory management is essential to any eBay seller's business. When buying and selling thousands of items per week, tracking inventory from source, to shelves, to shipment can be a monumental task. Many eBay businesses experience growing pains in this area because, as their sales increase, they neglect to upgrade their internal inventory management and end up selling items twice, shipping items that haven't sold, and even selling items they haven't yet purchased. These mistakes disappoint customers and quickly tarnish otherwise

"We work out of our home which is slowly becoming a warehouse. We have converted a large portion of our basement into a small warehouse for our inventory. We also have a section set up for packing and shipping our products."

—mrandjr

radiant feedback ratings. Before you start stocking your shelves, be sure that the inventory management strategy you have in place is sufficient for your current needs and will grow along with you.

Space Concerns

Your inventory storage facility must be large enough to hold your inventory comfortably, furnish a shipping department, a photography area, store extra shipping supplies, and allow room for growth. If you are planning on selling just a few items a month, this space might be only as large as the corner of your dining room. Many first-rate eBay businesses have started this way. However, as soon as you begin to develop regular sales, you'll need a facility more suited to your business needs.

Many of your toys and hobby items have special needs. They can be highly sensitive to their environments, and therefore you need to find, or build, a dry space with relatively ambient temperatures

> "With the vast number of toys I offered, I found that as I kept growing storing my inventory at home was not ideal. I ran an advertisement on craigslist.org asking for cheap storage spaces, and received many interesting offers. I found space through a friend who had an enormous attic space over a recording studio that he wasn't using. He rented it to me for close to nothing."
>
> —toysheik

and plenty of shelf space. Self-storage units are sometimes used because they offer security, climate control, and a low initial expense. However, they can sometimes be difficult to access after business hours, they don't leave much room for growth, and they often don't allow you to schedule regular shipping pick-ups from UPS or FedEx.

If you live in the city or suburbs, look around the industrial parks in your area. You may be able to rent a garage bay with ideal shipping capabilities for not too much more than a self-storage unit. Low-rent "behind-the-scenes" business parks make ideal locations for an eBay business. If you are out in rural locations, look around for some space in a local barn or warehouse.

Software

In Chapter 10 we outlined some auction management programs. All of these programs will help you track your auctions, from listing, to sale, to feedback, although some of them, such as ChannelAdvisor Pro, will also help you to track the flow of your inventory. A

"We have all of our listing sorted by toy line in our basement 'warehouse.' Each toy line is then broken down further by specific types of listings. Our smaller items are placed in individual sandwich bags with identification labels. All of these items are then stored in labeled protective clear drawers for easy locating during our packing and shipping process."

—mrandjr

good program will notify you when stock of a particular item is running low, will either re-list or restock items that failed to sell at auction, and will track your item sources and source expenses.

Layout

If you have the luxury of laying out the floor-plan of your storage facility, take "flow" into consideration. The best spaces allow for a continuous stream of inventory through the various stages of handling: logging new inventory, testing (if necessary), photography, shelving, and shipping.

If you have two bay doors, make one "in" for incoming inventory from your item sources, and make one "out" for shipments to customers. If you have only one bay door, send all incoming item shipments directly to a processing area where they are logged in to the management software, assigned an inventory ID code, and checked for accuracy and damage. Next, if you're dealing with

> "We have organized our inventory within two rooms of our home. Larger items are kept at another storage facility. We have plastic drawer bins that store our 'little store items.' We have a bookshelf for all our video games, books, and VHS tapes. We also have a separate room for our 'larger store items.' Once we've taken a photo of the item, it is placed back in it's place until sold."
>
> —pawpawrick

used inventory, shuffle it all to your testing area where you can make sure everything functions properly and is free of damage. Then, pass everything on to photography where the photos that you will need to use in your auctions are taken. If your auction management software doesn't already do this for you, create a photo database to keep track of which photos correspond with what items. For this purpose, have a networked computer set up at the photography station to make your job of listing auctions easier later. Once everything is photographed, you can stock it on your storage shelves while it awaits auction. Label your shelving system and stock your items according to the inventory ID that each item has been assigned, or by a similar cataloging system, so that when it comes time to ship an item, it will be easily located. Once an item has sold, send it off to the shipping department, and out the "out" door to the happy customer.

In the example above, managing a warehouse such as this sounds like enough work for a team of people. And while, ideally, it would be, many eBay sellers must make do with much less. To further organize the process and maximize the work of one or two people, many

> "Since most of our items are small, we mainly ship via First Class Mail from the USPS using bubble envelopes or small boxes that we purchase in large volumes. Larger items are shipped via Priority Mail using free packaging provided by the USPS."
>
> —mrandjr

PowerSellers assign a specific task to different days of the week. For example, on Sunday they devote the day to creating and submitting new auctions to eBay. On Monday, to ensure fast shipping to customers, they pack and ship all the items that have sold in the auctions that ended on Sunday. On Tuesday, they search for and purchase their inventory from the usual sources. On Wednesday, they log in and check all the new inventory shipments that have arrived at the warehouse since last Wednesday. On Thursday, they do the necessary photography, and on Friday they stock the items onto the warehouse shelves. Saturday might be a day off, but more likely, the day will be spent doing everything they couldn't finish up during the week. Of course, this schedule makes for a hectic week, but on the bare-bones budget of a new business, sometimes it is necessary.

> "I ship all over the world as far away as New Zealand, Peru, Brazil, Kuwait and Iceland. Years ago I would carry all my parcels to the post office, wait in line, and fill out all their forms. Now I take advantage of PayPal's integration with USPS and UPS. I can print labels from home and schedule pick ups. USPS even provides free shipping supplies for their Priority Mail service."
>
> —toysheik

Shipping

There are three main companies that sellers choose to handle their shipping: UPS, FedEx, or the US Postal Service. You will have to research which company works best for you in your area and location. The US Postal Service tends to be the least expensive, but you'll need to deliver packages to the post office every time you ship. UPS and FedEx are a little pricier, but will come to your door and pick up shipments. All three provide tracking numbers for your packages, which buyers always appreciate having.

When shipping internationally, be sure to fill out all the appropriate customs forms from whichever shipping company you choose.

CHAPTER 13

Finances

*W*ITH THE POSSIBILITY OF HUNDREDS OF TRANSAC-
tions per month, you will need to be diligent about tracking and recording your business's
finances. Not only will solid accounting practices help you at tax
time, they will also help you secure a bank loan, evaluate the health
of your business, and prove necessary when it comes time to sell
the company.

There are several ways to manage your business's finances. You
could take on the responsibility yourself, doing it either by hand or
in accounting software, or you could hire an accountant to help you.

If you're confident in your bookkeeping skills and have the time and energy to take on the task yourself, then by all means, you should. However, you shouldn't take on your own bookkeeping if you're not sure of yourself, if you don't have adequate time to do the job, or if you're just trying to save a few bucks. Doing a lousy job of bookkeeping will no doubt cost you more in the end than simply hiring an accountant up front.

Doing It Yourself

If you decide to take on the job yourself, you can easily find formidable help in the form of accounting software. There are a few great programs available that are designed to do exactly what you need. Luckily, if you accept most of your payments from buyers through PayPal, you will have easy access to a downloadable record of your received payments, which you can plug into the accounting software you choose. Also, if your auction management software allows you to track inventory, you should be able to export a list of all your inventory purchases as well. These two lists combine to compile an already formidable record of your business's finances. All you need to do is fill in around the edges with information such as your office and shipping expenses, income received from outside (non-PayPal) sources, rent, utilities, and so on.

Research the three programs that follow before you decide to depend on one. Some have downloadable demo versions that will allow you to evaluate the software for a period of time.

QuickBooks

Perhaps most well known is the business accounting program QuickBooks, from Intuit, the makers of Quicken. QuickBooks is available for both Mac and PCs, costs between $100 and $400 depending on the version, and releases an upgrade every year to stay current with tax information. For more information, visit www.quickbooks.com.

Money, Small Business

Microsoft's Money for small business is another widely used financial management application. It will help you manage your accounts, your spending, and your profit and loss reports through a simple interface. Money only runs on Windows XP or higher PCs and costs around $90. For more information, visit www.microsoft.com/money.

PeachTree

PeachTree's small business accounting software has been around and popular for many years. It is a robust accounting program specifically designed for small businesses. It, like Money, only operates on Windows PCs. It costs $199.95 and releases a new version every year. For more information, visit www.peachtree.com.

Business Vital Signs

The most important aspect of doing your own bookkeeping is to actually do it. Saving all your receipts and invoices for a rainy day during tax season will not help you to produce the quarterly, monthly, and weekly reports that you will need to make smart business decisions. You should be aware at all times of your company's vital signs, as indicated by your profit and loss statement, cash flow statement, and balance sheet.

Your profit and loss statement (P&L) should be easily produced from within your accounting software. It is simply a record of all your income and expenses over a given time period, usually a month. It will let you know whether you're business is profitable, and if not, where you need to make changes. Keep a file of previous months' P&Ls so that you can compare and track whether or not the changes you've made are working.

A cash flow statement simply tracks the money that comes into and goes out of your business. It can be used to track where your cash has gone, and to predict where your cash will be down the road. You should create a cash flow statement often enough that you are never side swiped by surprises. You need to know that you will have enough cash available to purchase next month's inventory. Otherwise, you'll be left with nothing to sell and no income.

A balance sheet measures all your assets (inventory, vehicles, cash, accounts receivable, etc.) against all your liabilities (loans, rent, accounts payable, etc.) and determines what your business is worth. Keeping a close eye on this report will let you know if your business is growing, or headed for failure. Generate this often for early signs of trouble.

Finding Help

You have quite enough to stay on top of, without trying to remain current on all the latest tax laws. Your time will be better spent watching for trends and innovations on eBay than watching for the latest IRS tax codes. Accountants can relieve you of a lot of stress, and therefore you should consider passing your accounting on to one of them.

Talk to other local businesses to find out who they trust for their accounting. If that search turns up empty, talk to your local SCORE chapter, your chamber of commerce, or your state's Small Business Association for recommendations. You'll want to interview several accountants before you enlist the help of one. Be sure to inquire into her work history. Has she been in the profession long? Is she a Certified Public Accountant? How much experience does she have accounting for small businesses? Solicit resumes. Ask for references. And then follow-through on calling them all. Your business will profit from your diligent research.

CHAPTER 14

Human
Resources

*T*HE DAY WILL COME WHEN IT IS NECESSARY FOR YOU
to start hiring employees. This chapter will
discuss how to know when that day has arrived
and what steps to take when it does. It will be a busy day, no doubt,
and you likely will feel stressed and anxious about taking the time
to find help amid your already hectic schedule. But take a deep
breath and relax. This is a necessary and exciting step to building a
business. Once you've got good employees behind you, your business will really start to take off.

When to Hire

Running an eBay business takes a lot of work. It requires long hours
in front of a computer screen, a lot of time on the phone, and some

stressful financial decisions. It is indeed a full-time job. But it should only be a full-time job. When the number of hours you work in a week creeps past 40 to 50 to 60 and worse, you should consider hiring some help. Remember, you started this eBay business to have more fun, take control of your schedule, and to free up some time. Didn't you?

If you find yourself working over 40 hours a week to keep up with the demands of the business, you should be in a position financially to afford one or two part-time employees. If you're not in a position to take on a few salaries, you should reassess the profitability of your business. Would it be more profitable to run less auctions at higher prices? Or, would the extra help be all that you needed to increase sales and cover the salaries? In either case, you should speak with your accountant about taking on help. He will be able to help you determine how much you can afford to pay, and whether or not you should offer benefits.

Before You Hire

Prior to hiring employees there are things you must do. New employees means new planning and new paperwork. The first step before you hire is to get yourself set up properly with the government.

Employer Identification Number

Up until this point, if you have operated your business as a sole proprietorship, you have not needed an Employer

Identification Number (EIN). An EIN is to a business what a social security number is to an individual. It simply identifies your business to the IRS and will be used when you withhold income taxes from your employee paychecks. To apply for your EIN, you will need to fill out, and submit, IRS Form SS-4. It can be downloaded from www.irs.gov/pub/irs-pdf/fss4.pdf.

Planning for Employees

Before you begin interviewing you should figure out where another set of hands would be most effective. What is the most time-consuming task in your day? Is it easily delegated to someone else or does it require your expertise? If you find yourself spending six hours a day shipping orders, you might consider hiring someone to take that on and free yourself up to generate more income for the business. Your time is best spent working on your business, not in it.

A helpful tool you can create is an employee map of your business. Draw out a job-tree placing yourself at the top as the boss. Below you, sketch the branches of your company: auction management, customer service, accounting, inventory management, shipping, and others. Within the branches, map out the individual jobs that you would need to make each branch run effectively. For each job you've mapped out, write a clear job description.

It may be years before your business is able to completely fill all the positions you've planned. But now is the time to begin filling them. Start with the jobs that can be easily filled and would most effectively free up your time. Then, work toward filling the ones that aren't as crucial but would make everything run more smoothly. In the beginning, you may need to hire one person for a few positions. But, because you've already written clear job descriptions, you can simply hand your new employee two or three descriptions and divide his week up accordingly.

Finding Employees

Finding people to apply for the positions you've created might be the easiest step in the whole process. Place an ad in your local papers, talk to friends and relatives, or put up fliers at the mall. Once you begin advertising your position, applicants will find you. Be aware of the markets in which you're advertising. If you're looking for an accountant, fliers at the mall will likely not yield legitimate results. If you're looking for a teenager to help part time with auction listings, advertise accordingly.

Screening Applicants

One of the largest problem areas for small business owners is troublesome employees. This is your chance to do all you can to weed out the potentially troublesome employees before you begin hiring. In addition to accepting the standard employment application—available at any local office supply store—make sure you also check references, proof of citizenship, conduct interviews, and do background checks. Hiring help will not help your business any if you end up with a thief in the middle of your stock room. Conversely, hiring the right people now may be exactly what your business needs to grow to the next level.

After You Hire

Now that you've got employees, your business is ready to roll. Or is it? There are still a few concerns that need your attention. Simply filling positions will not help a company run. Now you need to make sure your employees know what they're here to do, and you need to know what to do to take care of them.

More Paperwork

In addition to keeping your new employee's application, resume (if submitted), and references on file, you also need to collect some tax information from them. As the employer, you will be withholding income tax on your employee's paychecks. The amount you withhold is determined by the information your employee fills out on his Form W-4. You will need to keep a copy of Form W-4, and mail one to the IRS.

You must also ask your new employee to fill out IRS Form I-9, the Employment Eligibility Verification. To do this you will need a copy of the employee's passport, or driver's license and social security card. For a complete list of acceptable forms of identification, see the back of IRS Form I-9. You must keep every employee's Form I-9 on file for a period of three years from the hiring date. This form is not mailed to anyone.

Training

Spending time training your new employee thoroughly may seem like a nuisance and distraction now, but it will pay off for you in the long run. It is easier to train an employee well in the first two weeks than it is to be pulled away to help out your help every few minutes for six months. Provide your employee with the detailed job description you wrote at the beginning of this process. She will find it a useful guide when she has questions.

Taxes

FEDERAL INCOME TAX. As mentioned earlier, you need to withhold federal income taxes from your employees on every paycheck. The appropriate amount to withhold is determined by the tax information the individual employee supplies on his Form W-4. Use this information to find the appropriate amount in IRS Publication 15, Circular E, *Employer's Tax Guide*.

FICA. In addition to federal income tax, you must also withhold Social Security and Medicare taxes from your employees and pay a matching amount. At the time of this writing, the Social Security tax rate is 6.2 percent for all salaries up to $76,000, and 1.45 percent for Medicare.

FUTA. FUTA stands for the Federal Unemployment Tax Act, and it means that you need to pay more money. You pay 6.2 percent of the first $7,000 that your employee earns. However, you receive a credit for 5.4 percent of that on your own taxes. Use Form 940 or Form 940-EZ to file these taxes.

EMPLOYEE COMPENSATION. Along with all the paperwork above, you must submit to the IRS a report of employee compensation and withholdings, along with your share of the FICA taxes, on Form 941, *Employer's Quarterly Federal Tax Return.*

When you apply for your EIN, the IRS will send you a stack of Form 8109, the Federal Tax Deposit Coupon. If your total quarterly employment taxes are more than $500, you will need to file these taxes using Form 8109 every month before the 15th of the following month.

At the end of the year, you will need to provide your employees with their annual Form W-2s. This form, as I'm sure you know, summarizes earnings and withholdings for the year. You must deliver this form to all your employees before January 31st of the following year. You will need to keep a copy of all your employee's Form W-2s to file along with Form W-3 to the Social Security Association.

Yes, that's a lot of effort, math, and paperwork. For these reasons, many companies fill the accountant position first. If you find yourself stuck or confused by these tax requirements, you can do your own research at the following web sites:

- Social Security Administration (www.ssa.gov)
- Internal Revenue Service (www.irs.gov)
- Small Business Administration (www.sba.gov)

Or, you can find someone to help you at these sites:

- 1-800-Accountant (www.1800accountant.com)
- CPA Directory (www.cpadirectory.com)
- The National Association of Small Business Accountants (www.smallbizaccountants.com)

CHAPTER 15

Final
Thoughts

*W*ELL, THERE YOU HAVE IT—A CRASH COURSE IN
selling toys and hobby items on eBay. You
now know how to register on eBay, find items to
sell, create effective auctions, manage inventory, and hire help
when it's time! We've provided you with the best strategies for getting started, and the proven techniques for maximizing profitability.
Now it's up to you to become the next successful PowerSeller in the
world's largest marketplace.

Remember, selling on eBay will not always be easy. But you have
chosen to do it because selling toys is a fun way of life. That in itself
makes this venture more rewarding than any dead-end corporate

job anywhere. You have taken the reigns of your income and opened up your future to possibilities as limitless as eBay has proven, so far, to be. In time, you will learn more ins and outs of this marketplace than we could ever stuff into a pocket guide. Hopefully we've been able to set you on the right path to building a profitable business selling the toys you enjoy.

PowerSellers' Thoughts

As most sellers will tell you, there's more to eBay than profits, e-mail, and inventory. People do it for many reasons, most of them for reasons more meaningful than you would expect. Here are some closing thoughts about selling on eBay from some of our PowerSellers.

Customer Relationships

"Over time I have developed a lot of repeat customers, and I like hearing from them outside of eBay sales. In particular, I have a buyer in Australia named Rick. I have looked for items outside of my usual sources for him, and if he is looking for anything specific I will try to dig it up for him. To thank me, Rick once sent me a die-cast Ford Falcon race car that is sold in Australia. I really appreciated that gesture."

—Dale Shearer (maximum_thrash)

Hearing from Customers

"I enjoy selling magic. I've met some great people doing it. I love getting e-mails from customers telling me how much they enjoy performing their new tricks, or how their sons and daughters are having a ball performing these tricks for friends and family."

—Mike Garrido (MCMagic)

Selling Toys

"Selling on eBay has been very rewarding for us, both financially and emotionally. We know that when the items we sell are shipped off and arrive at their destination that there is a child (some young and some young-at-heart) waiting patiently to receive their new toy. We know that somewhere in the world we have put a smile on someone's little face."

—Richard Everman (pawpawrick)

eBay

"A few years ago I bought a book at a market called *The Good Citizen's Handbook: A Guide to Proper Behavior* by Jennifer McKnight-Trontz (Chronicle Books, 2001). When I read it I was working for a bank and thought to myself, 'Why can't I work in a place where people live and work by the values in this book?' After reading that, I came across eBay's Community Values and discovered why eBay was, and still is, becoming a worldwide phenomenon. With so much corruption these days in all levels of business and governments worldwide, it's easy for people to recognize eBay as a way of building communities and conducting honest business around the globe."

—Henry Pagan (toysheik)

The eBay Community Values:

- We believe people are basically good.
- We believe everyone has something to contribute.
- We believe that an honest, open environment can bring out the best in people.
- We recognize and respect everyone as a unique individual.
- We encourage you to treat others the way you want to be treated.

Good luck to you in your new adventure.

Index